Weight Training and Lifting

John Lear

A & C Black · London

First published 1989 by
A & C Black (Publishers) Limited
35 Bedford Row, London WC1R 4JH

© *1989 John Lear*

ISBN 0 7136 5674 3

British Library Cataloguing in Publication Data
Lear, John
   Weight training and lifting.
    1. Sports: Weightlifting – Manuals
    I. Title
    796.4'1
    ISBN 0–7136–5674–3

Photoset by Rowland Phototypesetting Limited,
Bury St Edmunds, Suffolk

Printed and bound in Great Britain by
The Bath Press Limited, Avon

CONTENTS

INTRODUCTION

This book is based upon the original British Amateur Weightlifters' Association Instructor's Handbook. The original was produced by the former National Coach, Alister Murray, and was the compilation of a series of articles written by him for national and international magazines. Some re-writing of this material was undertaken by Mr D. Harfield, the Treasurer and Staff Coach of the B.A.W.L.A. The essential material of these articles comprise the main section of this book.

New sections on Olympic lifting and Powerlifting have been added, as well as sections on training methods. It is now felt that the contents provide the coach and teacher with the essential basic knowledge to enable him or her to undertake the training of anyone in either of the sports of weightlifting or powerlifting. A comprehensive working knowledge of functional anatomy and kinetics related to the development of power through the use of weight training will also be gained.

The author is very grateful to all who have contributed over the years to the knowledge that is in this book. There is, however, very much more to be learned, but the information contained here should provide the student with the tools for a life-long study of a most fascinating subject. As such, this is an essential text book for anyone contemplating entering the B.A.W.L.A. coaching world. The coaching courses will give knowledge and ability and will provide good reason for what is taught. They will also encourage the student to weigh up the value of advice provided by others. Experience can mean little if one is unable to sift the wheat from the chaff.

Throughout the book coaches and lifters are, in the main, referred to individually as 'he'. This should, of course, be taken to mean 'he or she' where appropriate.

J. Lear B.A., Dip. P.E., Cert. ED.
Director of Coaching B.A.W.L.A.

OLYMPIC WEIGHTLIFTING

Mechanical considerations

The technique of weightlifting is based on the science of simple mechanics. The objective is to exert maximum force in the most efficient manner. To this end we are especially concerned with the following:

1 balance
2 line of least resistance

If these factors have been brought under the lifter's control, then he will be able to use his strength and speed in the development of maximum force in overcoming the inertia of the bar bell.

The positions that a lifter must pass through, especially during the pull, are often not those which would seem to be natural in overcoming a heavy weight. The problem, however, is that those movements which seem to be natural, such as leaning one's body weight against the resistance, lead to serious errors that cannot be corrected. It is, therefore, essential that correct technique should be understood and taught from the very beginning of a lifter's career. Remember, also, that the experienced lifter may fall into the errors that the handling of very heavy weights may present. Correct technique should not be sacrificed for heavy weights. Bad habits, once formed, often cannot be broken. Even after much correct coaching when the fault may appear to have been eliminated, there is always the danger that the lifter when under stress and pressure will revert to the first thing learned, i.e. the mistake.

There are two most important factors in the technique of any athletic exercise: these are balance and economy of effort (least line of resistance).

Correct balance

Body balance is a state of stability and control, with no strong tendency to move out of balance. To lose balance is to lose control. The mechanics of this are simple. *See Fig. 1.* This represents an upturned 56-lb weight, with the wide surface upwards. X is the centre of gravity, or centre of balance. The dotted line is the vertical line of balance which falls vertically through X and C, C being the weight-bearing centre and A to B being the base.

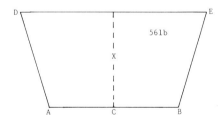

Fig. 1

A weight of 50lb is fixed to point D. The combined centre of gravity, X, of these two weights will now move outwards and upwards towards a point near D. X, the centre of gravity, will be outside the base, causing the two weights to over-balance as in Fig. 2.

In Fig. 3 a counter-balance of 50lb has been added to point E which will keep the 56-lb block back in its original position,

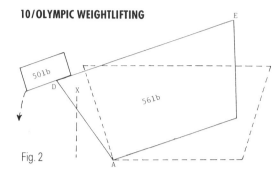

Fig. 2

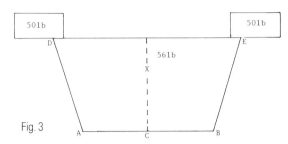

Fig. 3

except that the combined centre of gravity of the three weights will be higher up due to the position of the additional 50-lb weights. Remember, an object will remain in balance whilst its centre of gravity falls vertically within its base.

Line of least resistance

This can be found by the study of levers and fulcrums. (*See Fig. 4*.) 'P' is the power turning the lever, 'AF', at the fulcrum, 'F', to raise 'W', the weight, upwards through range A–B–C. By moving the weight from point A to X the lever, or weight arm, will be shortened; less power will then be required to raise the weight, or if the weight is left at point A, less power will be required to raise this weight through range B–C than through range A–B. For the same reason, the horizontal distance between 'W', the weight, and 'F', the fulcrum, will be less, thereby complying with this principle: 'as weight and fulcrum approach each other, resistance decreases'.

In weightlifting the long bones and spine are the levers, the points of power are where the muscles are attached to the bones and the fulcrums are the joints. Remember that in weightlifting the fulcrums must always be moved towards the resistance.

When talking in weightlifting terms about the snatch and clean, three basic stages of the lift are referred to:

1   the pulling position;
2   the transitional position;
3   the receiving position.

The pulling position and the receiving position are dynamic in the sense that the former requires great power to overcome the inertia of the bar and to develop acceleration, while the latter demands great control in a low and gymnastic position. The mastery of both require much skill and, therefore, considerable time should be spent with the young lifter, especially in mastering the techniques of these movements.

The transitional part of the lift refers to the actual change from pulling to the receiving position. The body is weightless as the feet leave the ground and at this time can therefore have little or no control over the direction or can participate in lifting the bar. The position through which the lifter goes will be very much controlled by the technique, satisfactory or otherwise, that has been adopted in the pull and this will consequently affect the final receiving position. It will be seen that whilst mistakes may manifest themselves in the receiving position, their origin will probably be in an error made at some stage of the pull (usually at the beginning). It is easy to see, for instance, that a lifter has dropped the bar behind the

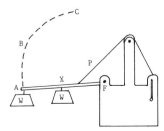

Fig. 4

head in the squat snatch. All of the audience will have seen this, but the good coach must be looking to see where the obvious error originated, and must be able to give *positive coaching advice* to eliminate the mistake at source.

To this end it is important that the coach has a blue print of correct technique in the back of his mind's eye against which he can see and measure every lift. The notes that follow are brief and concise. Study them carefully, especially those which are designated 'Key Positions'. When you are coaching, try to make sure that the lifter is passing through these positions at all stages of the lift.

The **key positions** are:
1 starting position – this refers to the exact moment when the bar leaves the platform
2 bar at knee height
3 full extension at the top of the pull
4 receiving position.

Remember, also, that a lifter may not pass through these positions properly because of any of the following:
1 lack of strength in any of the essential muscle groups working at any stage of the lift
2 loss of balance
3 use of the wrong muscle groups at the wrong time, i.e. lack of co-ordinated muscular effort
4 lack of full joint mobility
5 inability to develop speed as a result of no. 1.

These notes apply to the basic starting positions for all the lifts illustrated and described in this book. Please apply this description to all such positions, but remember that adjustments are applicable to the width of grip for the snatching illustrations.

Basic starting position (key position no. 1)

Feet	Approximately hip width apart, toes turned out slightly. Feel the weight of the body over the whole of the foot. This will ensure good balance.
Knees	The angle at the knees should be between 90–100 degrees.
Back	The back should be flat (this does not mean vertical).
Shoulders	The shoulders should be slightly in front of the bar.
Arms	The arms should be straight, but not locked rigid. They are described as being athletically straight.
Elbows	The elbows are turned out from the side of the body. This will ensure a more vertical pull.
Grip	*Clean and jerk* Basically, the grip for this lift will be just a shade wider than shoulder width.
Snatch The width of grip is decided by measuring the distance from elbow joint to elbow joint across the back when the arms are raised horizontally. This distance is then marked on the bar. The hands are spaced accordingly so that the marks lie between the first and second fingers.

Common points for both lifts

The hook grip should be used for all attempts. The head is tilted nearer to the vertical than the angle of the back. The eyes look at right angles to the angle of the head.

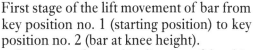

The squat snatch 1. Starting position

2. The bar is brought in towards the shins

First stage of the lift movement of bar from key position no. 1 (starting position) to key position no. 2 (bar at knee height).

Due to the forward inclination of the shin bone in the starting position, the bar bell is forward over the front part of the foot. This is too far forward for a correct lift: if it were lifted in a vertical line, the lifter would be pulled forwards to the front of his toes and consequently off-balance. The bar bell must, therefore, be eased back and into the shins as it is lifted from the floor so that by the time it is at knee height (key position no. 2) it is over the centre of the base of the lifter. This ensures that the lifter is in balance at a vital part of the lift and will consequently be able to exert maximum force as he passes, through this area of great resistance.

This is the only deliberate movement of the bar out of a vertical line of lift. The movement must be taught to all lifters from the beginning of their training.

The squat snatch

Photograph 1. See descriptions for starting positions. Snatch width grip.

Photograph 2. As the bar comes off the floor, it is eased slightly in towards the shins to bring the centre of the load over centre of the base. The shoulders will have moved slightly forwards in order to maintain a balanced position during the pull.

The bar has now moved slightly back and the head, shoulders and hips are lifted together.

The bar is still moving slightly backwards, but the head and shoulders are kept forwards. At this stage this is a major coaching point to prevent a backward pull.

The shoulders are still well forward. The bar is over the centre of the base, and the fulcrum of the shoulder is well in advance of the bar. This will help the long hip swing, because of the pendulum position of the bar and shoulders. This is key position no. 2.

2A

3. The upright position

Photograph 2A. The bar is now as far back as it should go. The knees bend as the hips are driven in and upwards towards the bar due to anatomical reaction. The head and shoulders move back only as a reaction to the forward swing of the hips.

The head is almost vertical over the bar. The lifter is still attempting to keep his shoulders in a pulling position over the bar. The bar should be travelling vertically.

Photograph 3. The body must be in an upright position of balance (most lifters have their shoulders too far back at this stage). The bar will be carried slightly forwards due to the hip swing. Note that the arms will still be athletically straight. This is key position no. 3. The extension is fully completed and the feet are just about to leave the ground. The bar is still travelling slightly forwards due to the hip thrust and the arms are still in approximately the same position, as the lifter should not attempt to bend the arms until the leg, hip and back extension nears completion.

The arm pull is now used to accelerate the lowering of the body. The forward movement of the hips is still being maintained to enable the hips to be lowered forwards under the bar.

The knees are turned outwards as the feet move apart. The bar is still rising on the momentum imparted by the terrific extension. The lifter should continue to direct the hip region forwards and downwards in an attempt to reach a vertical trunk position under the bar.

The lifter approaches the final receiving position beneath the bar by simultaneously performing the following movements. The bar is rotated within its own axis so that the heel of the hand is ready to drive the bar vertically upwards. The knees are opened and the hip region is pushed forwards and downwards.

Photograph 4. Here we see the lifter arriving in the lowest position possible beneath the bar. In this case, however, the bar has been directed slightly backwards and has

4. The lowest position beneath the bar

5. Start of recovery

6. The recovery

been checked by a slight forward movement of the head and shoulders.

Having checked the backward movement of the bar, the lifter is now in a position with the bar securely fixed. The upper trunk is nearly vertical and is in a perfect position of balance: the bar, shoulders and centre of base are in line.

The recovery

Photograph 5. To recover from the final low position of balance the lifter eases the head through the arms and simultaneously lifts the hips upwards. The arms remain nearly vertical, but there is a slight forward inclination of the trunk as the legs begin to extend. Midway through the final leg extension the trunk is brought back into the vertical position. The feet are stepped back into line to complete the lift.

The clean and jerk starting position

Starting position

The clean and jerk

The bar is gripped with the palms downwards and the hands are about shoulder width apart. The arms are straight, with the elbows rotated outwards. (Refer to the note on starting position.)

Photograph 1. The bar has been lifted from the platform, the lifter driving strongly with the legs, maintaining the angle of the back and keeping the shoulders in advance of the bar. The bar is eased back into the shins to maintain the combined centre of gravity of body and bar over the centre of the base. The arms are straight.

The bar is taken to knee height. This is key position no. 2. The lifter is evenly balanced over his feet, the bar is close to his knees and his shoulders are well forward.

As the bar passes the knees and lower thighs, the hips must be forced forwards and upwards towards the bar. Effort must be made to keep the shoulders forward as long as possible.

1. Key position no. 2

2. Maximum upward extension

2A. Full upward extension

3. Deep receiving position

3A

Due to the extension of the hip joint and the lifter rising up on his toes, the muscles which cause these actions also cross the knee joint and cause it to bend. This second knee bend is an anatomical action only. It is not a coachable point, but it is useful in that further extension of the leg gives added impetus to the top of the pull. Note that the lifter keeps his shoulders over the bar in an upward pulling position as long as possible. The arms are still straight.

Photograph 2. Here the lifter has reached the point of maximum upward extension and his feet are about to leave the platform. His shoulders are elevated and the arms are beginning to bend. This arm action is to accelerate the descent of the lifter under the bar and will not be effective in lifting the bar any higher.

The feet are jumped out to the side and apart, and the knees are also turned outwards. The position of the trunk, as achieved in full upward extension, must be maintained. The bending action of the arms is strongly emphasised as the lifter pulls himself down and under the bar.

As the feet come to land, the knees must be turned outwards; this will enable the lifter's hips to be placed close in between his heels, thereby maintaining an upward position of his trunk with his chest held high. The bar is rotated on its own axis and the elbows are brought up and under the bar to secure it on the chest.

Photograph 3. This is the deep receiving position of the squat clean. The hips are close between the heels, the knees are turned outwards, the trunk is upright, and the elbows are held high and forwards, securing the bar bell on the shoulders and clavicles.

To recover from the deep position the trunk is tilted slightly forwards whilst the elbows are kept high. By such an action the seat is lifted and pressure will be taken off the knee joint. This will enable the lifter to begin the straightening of the legs at the knees a little more easily. The knees must be kept turned out at all times as the lifter forces his way to an erect position. The feet are then stepped into line, in a hip-width position with the toes pointing fore and aft, prior to the jerk.

The jerk

Photograph 1. Having recovered from the deep squat clean, the lifter stands erect with his chest held high. Adjustment of the bar at the neck is permitted.

The jerk 1. Starting position

2. A balanced vertical dip

3. Driving high with maximum force

Photograph 2. The lifter dips his body vertically by bending at the knees. The depth to which he can dip whilst maintaining an upright vertical trunk is dependant upon the flexibility of his ankle joint whilst keeping his feet flat on the platform. It is essential that throughout the vertical dip the lifter is in balance. The elbows must be kept up to secure the weight on the top of the chest at all times during the movement. It is vital that this part of the movement is performed correctly. Success in the jerk depends upon correct technique.

Photograph 3. The lifter drives high, reaching up on his toes with maximum force. At the top of this drive the lifter splits off both feet, making sure that they come off the ground at exactly the same time, and drives upwards viciously with both arms.

The receiving position underneath the bar should be high, providing firm support for the weight above the head. The chest should be kept high so that the bar, shoulders and hip joints are in a vertical line of support over the effective centre of the base.

To recover from this position the bar bell is tilted slightly backwards and the front foot is stepped back a short pace. The rear foot is then brought into line. Great control must be exercised over each of the stages of this recovery.

The lifter remains motionless in the recovery position until signalled by the referee to replace the bar on the platform.

Learning the snatch

Since the snatch, or squat technique, is an unusual movement to start with, certain basic technical learning exercises can be used. These are listed in Chart 1 and should be followed in sequence; the lifter should not move onto the next stage until he has fully mastered the previous one.

Remember, it is important to try to teach the *squat technique* first. Most lifters will soon master this with a little attention to the exercises listed. If, after a reasonable attempt, it is not possible for the lifter to perform the squat technique, then the split may be taught.

The receiving position

SQUAT SNATCH-LEARNING EXERCISES

Bar	Feet	Action
1 On shoulders, behind neck	Receiving position	Press bar and sink into low receiving position
2 On shoulders, behind neck	Receiving position	Heave bar and drop into low receiving position
3 On shoulders, behind neck	Pulling position	Heave bar, jump feet to receiving position to drop into low receiving position
4 On top of chest	Pulling position	Heave bar, jump feet to receiving position to drop into low receiving position

VALUE (a) Learning the movements
(b) Mobility in low positions
(c) Balance and confidence in low positions
(d) Strength and power in receiving positions, e.g. 3 & 4 for Squat and 3 for Split are very important advanced exercises

Chart 1 Technical/leaning assistance exercises for the Snatch

Power assistance exercises

The Olympic lifts can be broken down into certain essential sections, and specific exercises to develop power within these areas are employed. The greater part of all training schedules will be made up of these power assistance exercises and this is especially so for the more advanced lifter.

Power assistance exercises can be divided into two types:

1 those which are very closely related to the complete Olympic movements and which are a vital part of these movements;

2 those which are general in their nature, i.e.

TECHNICAL EXERCISES	
Snatch	Clean
Power snatch	Power clean
Snatch balance	Clean grip pulls 100%
Snatch grip pulls 100%	Clean grip pull maximum
Snatch grip pull maximum	Clean grip shrugs
Snatch grip shrugs	Pulls from blocks
Snatch from blocks	(various heights; these exercises need
(various heights; these exercises need	very careful coaching)
very careful coaching)	Halting dead lift (clean grip)
Halting dead lift	Split squats
(snatch grip)	Front squats
RAW EXERCISES	
Power snatch without dip	Power clean without dip
Isometric pull in racks	Power cleans with dumb bells
Pulls to arms length with dumb bells	
Supporting heavy weights above the head	
TECHNICAL EXERCISES	
Jerk	General
Jerk balance	
Jerk from behind neck	
Jerk from racks	Short range power movements for pulls
Heave jerks	
¼ jerks	
RAW EXERCISES	
	Back squats
Jerks with dumb bells	Squat jumps
	Calf raises
Heave jerks with dumb bells	**Press** (military, seated, incline (bar bell
	or dumb bell))
Supporting heavy weights overhead	Round back good morning
	Selected muscle group/body building exercises
	Grip development; bench press (light)

Chart 2

(a) technical power assistance exercises, and

(b) raw power assistance exercises.

For our purpose power is a combination of strength × speed; therefore, all power assistance exercises are dynamic in the method of performance. The majority are highly technical and so they must be coached with the same attention to detail as the Olympic lifts. All too often they are left for the lifter to perform without coaching advice and, since the weights handled are, generally, considerably heavier than those that can be lifted in the Olympic movements, it is very easy to develop mistakes. Of course, the lifter then develops great strength in these mistakes which will seriously affect the performance of the Olympic lifts.

The chart opposite lists the major power assistance exercises.

It will be obvious that there are a great many more exercises than can be included in any schedule or programme. Selection of exercises will depend upon individual weakness, time of year, etc., but all schedules will usually include pulling and squatting movements of one type or another.

It is important to remember that the technique of these exercises must not be sacrificed for weight. This applies especially to pulling movements, for the nature of the pulling movement must be maintained and not changed into a dead lifting action.

The following are illustrations of some of the more essential basic power building assistance exercises. These exercises are high in technical elements and relate very much to the classical lifts. There are, however, many special muscle group exercises which it may be necessary to employ in training should weaknesses appear. These are illustrated under the sections on weight training.

High pull

Starting position

Feet should be hip-width apart, with the insteps under the bar. Bend the knees and hips and grip the bar with the knuckles to the front, hands shoulder-width apart. The hips should be higher than the knees and the back should be flat, with the shoulders slightly in advance of the bar. This is called the *get set* position. (*See photograph 1.*)

High pull 1. The 'get set' position

2. Maximum upward extension

Jerk balance 1. Starting position

2. Receiving position

Movement

Lift with the legs, maintaining the position of the back and head. As the bar passes the knees, force the hips forwards and upwards, reaching for a position of maximum upward extension. (*See photograph 2.*) Lower the bar to the starting position by bending the legs.

Breathing

Breathe in on the effort of lifting the bar and breathe out when lowering the bar.

Purpose

To build real power in the legs, back, shoulders and grip.

This exercise may be performed with a wide grip as for the snatch.

Jerk balance

Starting position

Assume the position shown in photograph 1. Make sure that the weight is evenly distributed over both feet and that the trunk is nearly vertical. The bar should rest solidly on the chest.

Movement

Bend both knees quickly, straightening the legs, and at the same time drive upwards with the arms and shoulders. As the bar clears the top of the head, place the front foot a short step forwards and dip the body by bending the knees to receive the bar in position. (*See photograph 2.*) Straighten both legs, then lower to the starting position.

Breathing

Breathe in as the bar is driven overhead and breathe out as it is lowered.

Purpose

To develop the skill and timing in jerking weights overhead and to develop power in this movement.

Split snatch balance press

Starting position
Assume the position shown in photograph 1, making sure you are perfectly balanced before you attempt to make your movement.

Movement
From this starting position, keeping the feet firmly in the same position, quickly bend and stretch the legs. At the same time drive the bar slightly forwards and upwards with the arms. Now dip the body as the bar passes the forehead, lowering into the position shown in photograph 2. This position is known as the *receiving position*.

Split snatch balance press *Above* 1. Starting position.
Below 2. Receiving position

Note that the trunk is vertical and the knee of the front leg is pushed well forwards over the ankle. Try to sit on the forward heel without the rear knee touching the floor.

Breathing
Breathe in prior to starting the movement.

Purpose
To assist in teaching the split style snatch, and to develop mobility, co-ordination, power and confidence that are essential in learning this lift.

Squat snatch balance press 1. Starting position

2. Receiving position

Front squat 1. Starting position

2. Full squat position

Squat snatch balance press

Starting position
Assume the position shown in photograph 1, making sure that the feet are turned outwards.

Movement
Dip the body by bending both legs to lower the bar a few inches. Immediately rebound from this shallow knee bend by extending the legs and arms to send the bar upwards. Drop under the weight, as shown in photograph 2, by bending the knees into a full squat. It is important to force the knees outwards and to keep the trunk upright.

Breathing
Breathe in prior to starting the movement.

Purpose
To assist in teaching the squat style snatch, and to develop the qualities of mobility, co-ordination, power and confidence which are essential in learning this fine athletic lift.

Front squats

Starting position
Load the barbell on the squat stands. Grip the bar, bend the knees and raise the bar clear of the stands. Step back from the stands. Place the feet hip-width apart, with the toes turned out. Keep the elbows high throughout the movement.

Movement
Lower the body into the position shown in the second photograph. Vigorously extend the legs and, keeping the chest high and the back flat and upright, return to the standing position.

Breathing
Breathe in before you bend your knees, and breathe out as you rise to the standing position.

Purpose
Mainly to develop the muscles on the front of the thighs and the hip muscles.

Split squats

Starting position
Take up the position shown in photograph 1 (p. 26). Make sure that your balance is perfect before attempting the movement.

Movement
Lower the body and the weight from the first position to the second position by bending both legs. Note how the forward knee is in advance of the forward foot. Straighten both legs to the starting position.

Breathing
Breathe in prior to starting the movement and breathe out as you rise.

Purpose
To build power and mobility in the legs in the receiving position employed in the split clean.

Power cleans with barbell

Starting position
Assume the position shown in photograph 1 (p. 26). The legs are well bent, but the back is flat.

Movement
Extend the legs and back vigorously, bringing the arms into action as the bar passes the knees. Finish in the position shown in the second photograph.

Breathing
Breathe in as you lift, and breathe out as you lower the bar to the starting position.

Purpose
To develop all-round body power. This is a major power exercise.

Split squat 1. Starting position

2. Full lunge position

Power cleans with barbell 1. Starting position

2. Receiving position

Squat–deep knee bend 1. Starting position

2. Full squat position

Squat – deep knee bend

Starting position
Feet are comfortably apart, normally hip width, and the toes are turned out slightly, with the bar resting across the upper back.

Movement
Bend the knees and squat down low. (*See photograph 2.*) Gently rebound out of his position and rise strongly by lifting the head; at the same time strongly straighten the legs.

Low position
The back is kept flat, but no vertical. This position elevates the ribs and has a stretching effect on the thorax, which encourages chest growth.

Breathing
Fill the lungs, bend the knees and breathe out as you rise.

Purpose
To develop the legs, back and chest, and to improve the condition of the respiratory and circulatory systems. This is a major exercise in weightlifting power development.

Power snatch

Starting position
Adopt the starting position as for the snatch. (*See photograph 1.*)

Movement
Drive vigorously with the legs, keeping the bar in as for the snatch. As the bar passes the knees, force the hips forwards and upwards, reaching as high as possible. As the position of maximum extension is reached, pull the bar high above the head to catch it at arm's length with a slight dip of the body.

Breathing
Breathe in at the start of the movement and breathe out when lowering the bar.

Purpose
To develop real power in the legs, back, shoulders and grip. This is a very dynamic

Power snatch 1. Starting position

2. Receiving position

Power jerk 1. Keep the chest and elbows up

2. Receiving position

movement and is a major assistance exercise for the snatch.

Power jerk

Starting position
Lift the bar onto the top of the chest. Keep the elbows up and the chest high. The feet should be hip width apart.

Movement
Keep the chest high and the elbows up. Keeping the feet flat on the floor, bend the knees. From this position drive vertically high on to the toes, thrusting the bar to arm's length. Dip the body to catch the bar. Try to drive high and to lock out strongly.

Breathing
Breathe in prior to the dip and breathe out as the bar is locked above the head.

Purpose
This is a very dynamic exercise to develop great power for the jerk.

Training plans and programmes

Fundamental questions

The selection of schedules and training plans has, for many years, presented the weightlifter with a major training problem. 'How do I train?', 'When do I train?', 'What combination of exercises should I use?' and 'Should I concentrate on power building, technique or fitness training, and how are these to be arranged within a training plan?' are questions always in the mind of the athlete. It is hoped that this section will help the lifter find the mainstream of the many varied ideas that exist and will show, by careful attention to the build-up of progressive training methods, that success can be achieved and that the overall standard of lifting can be improved.

In an involvement with any activity it is essential that the participant has a philosophy in which he can believe. Such a philosophy must always incorporate the desire to be the best. This quality alone will go a long way in helping to overcome the difficulties and inevitable setbacks that occur in a lifting career. The lifter must understand the sport thoroughly and all the requirements necessary for success. Such knowledge will help prevent wasting time on unnecessary activity. The term 'fitness' must be understood and what it means in relation to the sport; once this knowledge has been assimilated, it must be used intelligently.

Success breeds success at all levels. Even the greatest champions begin their careers by competing in and winning comparatively minor competitions. These early triumphs are the inspirations for further endeavours. They become the buttresses of the lifters' philosophy and are the strengtheners of their determination. Let us consider the philosophy in a little more detail.

Fitness for weightlifting

The first consideration can be posed in the question, 'Are you fit to be a successful weightlifter?'. Even this question at the outset contains the qualification of success. Anyone can lift weights. Many people do so for recreational purposes alone and one must not decry the pleasure that they derive from such participation. In our context, however, success applies to winning – to pushing oneself to the limits of personal ability. What, then, is our special fitness? It is *the ability to perform the activity of weightlifting with success and to be able to recover quickly*. Let's see how this definition can be applied to the sport and the essential steps necessary to make it viable.

Strength
It is important to develop great strength. This is what the basis of weightlifting is all about. No weak lifters are champions. Fortunately, this is perhaps the easiest aspect of the activity and in the sport the sky is

the limit as far as strength development is concerned. Most of the lifters are much stronger than their technical ability will permit them to show.

Speed
The quality of speed is the ultimate end product of all major athletic events that are not judged on aesthetic presentation. Weightlifting is an explosive activity. Maximum force needs to be generated in the shortest possible time. This means that the quicker you can bring into effective play the great strength that you develop, the greater will be your power.

Power
In weightlifting terms power is force (strength) multiplied by velocity (speed). Power is the most important factor in the successful accomplishment of all weightlifting and other athletic events of an explosive nature. Together with strength, the quality of speed can be developed and at certain times in the training plan this should be given special attention.

Fitness
In preparing a plan and corresponding schedule of work, the lifter often gets carried away by grand ideas of workouts that time proves him incapable of completing. The reason why he will be unable to fulfil his best intentions will be his lack of fitness for the work load that he has set himself.

Actual physical fitness is very hard to define, because it varies considerably from activity to activity. The marathon runner could not be expected to lift the heavy weights handled by the lifter, or the lifter to run the marathon, so the fitness requirements will be seen to be different. In our original definition we talk of being able to recover quickly. This means: *having undertaken to train at a certain load level, it is essential that the lifter can recover quickly enough to be able to repeat his training at a* *similar or greater load at subsequent training sessions.* Often the best laid plans will fail because the lifter cannot recover quickly enough from one workout to another.

Strength is developed by resistance to overload; general physical fitness is achieved by physiological overload. This simply means that the systems of the body, which involve heart, lungs and circulation, are stimulated to greater efficiency by subjecting them to levels of work over and above those normally necessary for the ordinary living process. In books on physical education these systems are referred to as cardio-vascular (heart and circulation) and circulo-respiratory (efficient use of oxygen and expiration of carbon dioxide). Since much weightlifting training (training for power) necessitates the use of heavy weights and, consequently, low repetitions, placing heavy overload on the muscular system only, little is done to develop cardio-vascular and circulo-respiratory fitness. The efficiency to a high degree of these systems is essential in the work recovery cycle and, therefore, is vital in successful progress planning.

In physiological terms much of the training for weightlifting is of an anaerobic nature (muscle work without direct oxygen supply from breathing), but for maximum efficiency work of an aerobic type (with direct oxygen supply from breathing) is also needed.

Coaching
In coaching the sport a great deal of attention is always paid to the mastery of the techniques of the lifts, and a sound understanding of the principles of mechanics is essential. In weightlifting the movements of the two lifts are difficult and unusual, and it is especially important to remember that they are to be applied to a 'changing apparatus'. (By this is meant that there is a considerable difference between a first

attempt clean and jerk, with a weight that should be overcome comparatively easily, and a third attempt which may well be a personal or even a national or world record. The apparatus has effectively been changed. This change can disturb a lifter psychologically and thereby can cause technique to break down. The activity of weightlifting is therefore complex.)

Training schedules must always include work related to the maintenance and development of correct technique. This technique must be reinforced constantly by correct practice of the lifts and the application of technical assistance exercises. At the extreme range of stress, the big championship, skill must not let the competitor down. It is not the object of this section to discuss the actual techniques of the lifts, but attention to the value of the assistance exercises will be paid in subsequent sections and schedule plans.

Involved with technical training is the necessity for full range mobility in all joint complexes. This flexibility is essential in the mastery of technique and thereby the full exploitation of the other qualities for which weightlifters train.

Willpower and motivation

Reference has been made to the great desire to be the best. The culmination of his desire can be reinforced by many forms of motivational methods. Motivation can be achieved through external rewards, such as money, houses, cars, improved job and family prospects and so on, but since such are unlikely to come the way of weightlifting athletes, the motivating factors that make the champion must come from within. It is easy to lose heart and if one's philosophy is not balanced, incorporating the basic foundations referred to previously, one's chances of success will be limited.

Determination and single-mindedness of purpose are the cornerstones of the strength of character that is needed by the champion. He must be prepared to work very hard for many years and to overcome the setbacks of injury and defeat. The famous American lifter, Pete George (American and World Champion as a teenager), said, 'Anything you want badly enough you can get. Burning desire or enthusiasm is the motivating force that can make a man a champion.' Most people who achieve greatness have an innate advantage, but it is only by using their natural talents to the full and by working very hard that they reach the top of their chosen field of activity.

Sport is a natural part of man's development. Man is always striving to conquer, to establish himself as the prime living creature. Much progress in the history of mankind has been dependent upon his intelligence and search for knowledge (and its practical application). The development of scientific weightlifting is in its infancy. Consider what the records may be in 100 years' time. Man's development in weightlifting, as in other sporting fields, depends upon the removal of inhibition. This is achieved by repeatedly submitting oneself to suitable stressful situations within the training context and by overcoming them successfully. These conditions exist in both *training and competition*. The training plan and schedules must be arranged to overcome such situations. They must be designed to master appropriate stressful situations and not to create conflicting stress through misapplication or too hasty advancement.

Summary

Our philosophy can be expressed, therefore, in the need for:

1 the development of great strength
2 the development of speed and athletic ability

THE TRAINING PROCESS ANALYSED

Problems	Facts	Dangers	Requirements
One has to choose from many schedules which may be unscientific or individualistic.	Overload on an organ of the body can produce either training or collapse (Folbort, USSR, 1958).	Overtraining – not enough rest and recovery.	Development of great power.
Unrealistic appraisal of one's ability in terms of effort and performance.	Continual progression over long periods without breaks is inconsistent with training process.	Undertraining – too much rest means there would be no training of the organ.	Development and maintenance of levels of skill.
Problems may be either physiological or psychological, or both.	Adequate recovery must follow work for the training process to occur.	The schedules of champions must not be copied by reducing weights used.	Development of physical fitness related to heavy work loads.
Other problems, internal or external, to lifter.	The load, volume and intensity require variation and control.	Without physiological robustness work load must be low, resulting in little progress.	Development of willpower.
		Weaknesses must receive attention. Training solely on one's strengths is unbalanced training.	A desire to be the best. This is best achieved by successful progression.
		Mental strain of prolonged competition stress can cause disastrous physiological changes.	Detailed personal attention: Diet – adequate and varied food intake. Sleep – sufficient rest/recovery. Stress – alleviate undesirable pressures.

Chart 3   The training process analysed

3 the development, as a consequence of 1 and 2, of great power
4 the development of systematic fitness and physical hardness
5 the mastery of technique
6 the desire to be the best, reinforced by motivating factors.

Training of junior weightlifters

The training of junior weightlifters falls into two categories: those classified as school boys in the age range 13–16 years, and those following through to the junior age limit of 20 years.

It is felt that some guidance must be given in the training and preparation of junior lifters in both of these categories in order to establish a sound basis for progression at senior level. Recent observation of lifters, especially in the school boy classification, highlights three concerns.

1 Advisability for a process of selection of boys for weightlifting

Under this heading we are concerned with the results of selection procedures which will determine whether a boy may be:

(a) suitable to take part in the sport, or
(b) less suitable to take part in the sport.

It must be pointed out here that those falling into the 'less suitable category' should not be discouraged from participating in the activity, but it must be remembered that they are unlikely to achieve high results, as they mature, even under the most favourable training circumstances. Much intrinsic enjoyment, however, will be likely to accrue for such people by participating in the sport and often many such people make up a large proportion of those taking part in the sport who operate at a club level.

In general terms, those boys showing high levels of ectomorphy and, to a lesser degree, endomorphy will be considered less suitable than those with mesomorphic characteristics. Similarly, boys who are tall and gangly, i.e. without commensurate muscle mass, will also ultimately be at a disadvantage. In early stages, advantages that such boys achieve through the mechanical principles of angular momentum will, subsequently, be lost with maturity.

Boys in the suitable group will tend to be short in height and will display the general characteristics associated with mesomorphy. In addition, an aggressive temperament and a will to win should be looked for. These latter two psychological requirements may also be found in those described as unsuitable and may tend to overcome, to some degree, physical failings in the early stages. Generally, the suitable group should additionally display the following anthropometric measurements/requirements.

General physique appearance

They should be somewhat shorter in height for their bodyweight than the average boys of similar age. This applies especially to those classes in the bodyweight classification 100kg and below. The 110kg group and 110+kg group will show a greater height range with the greater body mass. Broadness of shoulders, depth of chest and sturdiness in the waist area are also required. A slight tendency to fatness, whilst indicating a possible lack of physical condition, should not be considered a serious handicap.

Flexibility

Flexibility in the major joint complexes is essential and whilst it is possible to train for this quality, especially with the youngest lifters, it is of great value if the following major areas show basic essential ranges of movement:

(a) extendibility of the elbow joint to a minimum of 181°

(b) hyper-extendibility at the arm, and at the shoulder (arms above the head whilst keeping the trunk still and upright), to a minimum of 185°

(c) dorsi-flexion of the ankle, maintaining the foot on the floor; the boy should be able to sit in the full squat with the upper two-thirds of his trunk in an upright position

(d) extension of the hip joint as per the receiving position for the jerk, with the body maintained in a vertical position; the angle of extension at the hip joint should be to a minimum of 15°

(e) consideration of the size of hand and length of fingers and thumb; ability (or potential ability) to hook grip the bar.

Note on flexibility

It is important to realise that whilst minimum measurements are given, these are in reality the most for the performance of the skill of lifting and any extension of these measurements beyond those suggested will be in the region of 1–2° only. This will be found to be of benefit in the development of technical aspects of the sports. Hyper-extendibility beyond these measurements will have the opposite effect and will be liable to reduce the effectiveness of the lifter.

It is important, however, that flexibility is maintained throughout the lifter's career as per the requirement of the classical movements, rather than extended by specialist exercises. Over-flexibility in the joint complexes mentioned could result in unsuitability.

It will be found that once sufficient flexibility, in relation to the classical movements, has been developed it will be maintained by the correct employment of technical assistance exercises which fit in the general training programmes.

Explosive requirements (strength × velocity)

Olympic weightlifting is one of the most demonstrative displays of power in sport and requires the ability to overcome great resistance with maximum speed. To this end those boys who show ability to act quickly and with great force should produce favourable results. The following tests can be used as indicators of power:

1 20-metre dash from lying start
2 60-metre dash from standing start
3 2-handed throw with shot back over the head
4 standing long jump off two feet
5 standing high jump off two feet (this exercise may be measured through the Sergent jump test)
6 front squat; this exercise has been selected for two reasons:
    (a) it is safe for the participant to perform, because in the case of danger the bar bell can be dropped off forwards;
    (b) its relationship is very close biomechanically to the classical exercise.

After sufficient time has been given for the participant to acclimatise himself to the technicalities of the front squat movement, the ability to squat with bodyweight should be achieved easily.

Summary

It is hoped that by bearing in mind these considerations, both morphological and power, the coach will be able to select boys for the activity of weightlifting who will develop rapidly and gain great satisfaction from their success.

It should be remembered that those boys who fit the descriptions shown above often find themselves unsuitable for many activities, especially those of a games nature which make up the bulk of the physical education in schools. Such boys are often short in stature, and so weightlifting is an ideal activity for them.

It is important to remember, of course, that those who do not fit into this category may also derive much pleasure from the sport and that they should not be discouraged from taking part.

2 Technical development: major concern with young lifters

The correct technical development of young lifters is of the greatest importance and it is in this area that the coach has the greatest responsibility. Any motor skills that are learned at the very earliest stages of any sport will be the ones that will remain with the athlete, either consciously or subconsciously, for the rest of his career.

Should the young lifter be allowed to develop incorrect technical habits, it will be very difficult to eradicate these during subsequent training stages, despite the fact that technical errors may apparently be eliminated through careful coaching. It is the experience of this author that lifters, even of the highest grading, will revert to those errors that were first learned when they find themselves in stressful situations, such as competition at the highest level.

It is important, therefore, to repeat the fact that coaches have a great responsibility to ensure that the correct technique is taught from the very earliest stages and that principles should not be sacrificed by allowing the young lifter to handle weights which are too heavy for him at the beginning of his career.

It is now accepted that the advantages lie with the squat technique of snatching and cleaning and this should be followed wherever possible. Both coaches and lifters must persevere, although at the early stages when the lifter is young no problems should, in fact, be encountered in mastering the squat technique of lifting.

Generally speaking, it is a waste of time for the young lifter to be taught the split technique unless, after considerable effort, it is deemed that he will not be able to master the squat style. A considerable amount of time should be spent in the mastery of technique by employing technical assistance exercises in its build-up. For the jerk, the split technique must be taught.

The teaching of the Jerk from the shoulders is of special importance here. This may be the first exercise to be taught to the lifter for the following reasons:

(a) it gives the young lifter a sense of achievement in lifting weights above the head, which he will undoubtedly see as the objective of his participation in the sport

(b) it will help to develop strength in the arms and shoulders, which is the area naturally weaker than other muscular parts of the body in the beginner

(c) mobility must be developed in the hip region, with special emphasis given to the relationship of the pelvis to the rear leg in the split position. The extension of the rear leg backwards is an area of flexibility which is not catered for in the squat technique and associated assistance exercises.

In all squatting movements the hip joint is flexed rather than extended. Additionally, there is a tendency in both squat snatching and squat cleaning to push the chest forwards in the final receiving position. This movement results in a curvature of the lumber spine, with the hips being tilted backwards. Whilst such a position of the trunk is acceptable in the technique of the snatch and clean, a similar position does not afford the best support or position of balance when handling heavy weights in the jerk above the head.

It is essential, therefore, that the young lifter is introduced to this movement through the jerk balance exercise and that some time is spent on the teaching of the movement from the very earliest stages. Some coaches have criticised this exercise as being very difficult to teach. The author cannot agree, provided the exercise, as recommended, is one of the first to be taught. The exercise only becomes difficult to perform when it has to be used as a remedial exercise for the more advanced lifter when he has already developed some postural defect in his supporting position for the jerk.

In addition to this exercise, lunging movements during the free standing warm-up and 'split squats' with the bar on the front of the chest may be performed to improve flexibility and strength in the split receiving position of the jerk. Further to the development of the jerk, the heave jerk exercise should not be introduced too soon, as this exercise tends to cause the lifter to arch his lower back, setting his seat back and his chest forward as he receives the bar overhead. This movement can encourage incorrect technical position if used too soon in the lifter's technical development.

Remember that at all levels the majority of failures on the clean and jerk occur in the jerking movement and in most instances these failures occur, not through lack of strength, but through the lifter being in an incorrect technical position to support the weight above his head.

Apart from the emphasis on the jerk position, technical development should be ensured by following a build-up procedure for mastery of the complete skills of snatching and cleaning. This should be done in the following ways.

Snatch
The snatch balance exercises should be used to build up the skill, flexibility and strength necessary to achieve the effective receiving position and the lifter should not be allowed to progress throughout those exercises until mastery has been achieved stage by stage. These exercises are described elsewhere and should be well-known to all coaches, but they are included here in brief note form.

1 Feet in receiving position, bar behind neck; press and sink into low receiving position.
2 Feet in receiving position, bar behind neck; heave and sink into low receiving position. (This is a more dynamic version of the first exercise.)
3 Feet in pulling position, bar behind neck; heave, jump feet to receiving position and drop into final receiving position. (Similar exercises can be employed for the split technique lifters, but since the emphasis is upon squat technique these will not be described here.)

In addition to these exercises, the lifter should be taught how to lift the bar from the starting position to full extension through various stages of the pull.

(a) Lifting the bar from the floor to knee height, easing it back in to the shins as the legs straighten and keeping the shoulders forward with the elbows rotated out, arms straight.
(b) Driving of the hips forwards into the bar as it passes the knees and lower thighs.
(c) Elevation of the shoulders upwards as the lifter rises onto his toes, allowing the arms to bend slightly.

The lifter must be conscious of the positions that he should be passing through. In conjunction with the snatch balance exercises, this pulling movement is extended to the beginnings of the receiving position with the bar above the head. This is the power snatch.

Clean
The squat technique will be taught and the front squat exercise which has already been considered to be an important exercise for the basic selection process will become an important part of the training programme. Again, pulling positions employing the clean width grip should follow stages as described for the snatch and can subsequently lead to the power clean and the full squat clean.

Jerk
The jerk from the shoulders should be taught through the jerk balance exercise, taking light weights from stands on to the chest to perform this movement. In addition, the dip and drive for the jerk should also be taught, ensuring that the lifter fulfils the following technical requirements.

Dip The trunk is maintained upright; elbows are kept high, securing the bar on top of the chest. The dip is vertical, maintaining the feet flat on the floor. (Depth to which this dip can be performed depends upon the flexibility of the ankle joint whilst maintaining the trunk upright and keeping the feet flat on the floor.) The elbows must not drop.

Drive The trunk is maintained in a vertical position. The lifter drives high up onto his toes; elbows must be maintained in position and should not be allowed to drop.

Split The lifter must split off both feet together. He must be taught to 'stay high' in the receiving position. He will be familiar with this position through initial practice of the jerk balance exercise.

These descriptions of technique training are very basic. However, it must be emphasised that these basics are essential in the development of technique and that they cannot be avoided if weightlifters of a high calibre are to be produced with limited technical problems when they reach the 'real weightlifting' age between 19–25. It is during this period that greatest progress must be made and the emphasis will then be on power training.

It will not be to the advantage of the experienced lifter to have to keep modifying his training programme in order to try to compensate for technical disturbances which should never have been permitted to develop in the first instance.

Ideas behind the training plan

13–16 years age group

In many cases this is the time when enthusiasm will be high. The boy will be very receptive and he will, no doubt, see himself as a future World, or Olympic, champion. He will be prepared to work very hard and very often. (Coaches can use the strongest schoolboy clean and jerk contest as an initial objective.)

This in itself is not bad, but it is essential that the unbounded enthusiasm should be carefully directed. If it is not, then progress will be limited and it is likely that a boy will be lost to the sport. If his efforts are non-productive, there are many other distractions to take him away. His training, therefore, needs to be disciplined, effective and progressive.

It is essential that a broad base of physiological robustness is laid so that the boy may be 'weightlifting fit' enough to tackle the heavy programmes that he should be following in his late teens.

Early training should include:

1 general fitness training, and
2 specialised fitness training.

General fitness will involve the lifter in all forms of games, swimming, running, field athletics and gymnastics, the latter two being of special value.

Special fitness will centre around short duration/explosive work: sprinting, jumping, throwing and specialised (non-ballistic) flexibility work.

Sequence technique has been dealt with already, and power exercises should be technique-related and very carefully coached. Do not allow weight to break down technique. Bad habits are very difficult to break in strength activities, and under stressful conditions the lifter almost inevitably reverts to the habits first acquired, usually with disastrous results.

I explained earlier that the young boy will be full of enthusiasm, so some control must be exercised over the amount of time devoted to training. Generally, it should be restricted to three times per week with weights, especially for the first two years of this age group. It can be extended to four times at 15–16 years, but remember that additional fitness training should be worked at as well.

Boys should follow through the schools scheme leading to the National Championships. It is essential that:

1 the boy can measure, and take pleasure in, his success and consequent motivation

2 at this stage the coach should take pride more in how the boy lifts than in the amount he can lift

3 both the coach and the young lifter move progressively, and successfully, from one realistic aim to another

4 the coach has a responsibility to guard against the destructive effects of over-motivation from within the boy, from his parents and from the coach himself

5 the coach should remember that the young lifter is not a man, either physi-

cally or mentally, even though he may think he is and that he will have many problems associated with growing up: physiological, endocrinological, psychological and the sheer physical amount of school work, examinations, etc. that he is expected to cope with.

All these can affect the young boy, but if he gets through them the next stage will provide him with the real meat of his sport.

16–20 years age group

The lifter will move through adolescence into manhood. This is another period with many difficulties for him to overcome, but his capacity to handle heavy lifting sessions will increase with the steadily increasing characteristics of masculinity. To this end programmes will develop according to the following:

1 a gradual reduction in the amount of training time devoted to fitness
2 an increase in the amount of time devoted to the development of power
3 continuous technical reinforcement by the coach (guard against delusions of grandeur, should the lifter prepare his own training plans)
4 selection of competition and careful competition build-up to ensure progress
5 related to no. 4: selection of competitions which provide increasing challenge to develop psychological hardness under stressful conditions.

In addition, the good coach should understand how to deal with problems, rewards and punishments. Remember, it is not just the job of the coach to be the 'nice guy' all the time. It may be necessary for him to deal with the problems associated with adolescence and often this is unpleasant both for the coach and for the lifter.

Training of the novice lifter

The twin aims are to acquire power and skill.

Development of power: this is best achieved by employing those exercises closely related to the classical lifts. These are largely massive and dynamic in nature.

Development of skill: this is best achieved by the repetitive practice of those specially designed assistance exercises aimed at the development of the complete technique.

Stage 1

It is recommended that the novice lifter trains three times a week, with each workout followed by a day's rest: e.g. training days 1, 3 and 5 and rest days 2, 4, 6 and 7. The coach has to assess carefully the training weights, emphasising skill rather than heavy weights. Forcing is to be avoided at this stage.

Opposite is a typical example of first stage schedules for a novice lifter.

Schedules should be rounded off with exercises for the trunk, e.g. lower back or abdominals (3 sets × 10 reps). Also included should be exercises for all joint complexes, to maintain and develop full range of mobility, and a short period of light running. Use the split squat to develop hip mobility.

So that good motor habits are formed, the weight of the bar should not be increased for several sessions. When technique has developed and improved, small additions can be made gradually. Eventually the ascending bar principle can be introduced.

Stage 2

Progression can now be made to a second stage. An alternate schedules system may be used and can be applied in the following way: training day 1 – Schedule A; training day 2 – Schedule B; training day 3 –

TRAINING DAY 1

Exercise	Sets	Reps
Warm up (running, free-standing exercises, mobility exercises)	5	5
Power clean	5	5
Snatch balance exercise	5	5
Snatch pulls	5	5
Back squat	5	5

TRAINING DAY 2

Warm-up		
Power snatch	5	5
Jerk balance exercise	5	3
Clean pulls	5	5
Front squats	5	5

TRAINING DAY 3

Warm-up		
Continuous clean and heave press	5	5
Snatch balance exercise	5	5
Clean – squat	5	3
Dumb-bells press	5	5

SCHEDULE A

Warm-up	
Snatch	5×5
High pull)	2×5
Clean grip)	1×4
)	2×3
Jerk balance ex.)	5×3
Front)	2×5
Squats)	3×3

SCHEDULE B

Warm-up	
Clean and Jerk	5×3
High pull)	2×5
Snatch grip)	1×4
)	2×3
Snatch balance ex.	5×3
Back squat	5×5

Schedule A; training day 4 – Schedule B; and so on. This is an example of a programme that may be followed.

Schedules should be rounded off with trunk exercises, flexibility exercises for all joint complexes and a short period of jogging.

After some 6 to 10 weeks, depending upon the individual's progress, a total should be made in competitive conditions. From the results of this competition the lifter's best snatch and clean and jerk will be known. These results will be used by the coach to calculate his future training loads in the ensuing intermediate stage.

Training lifters of intermediate qualification

Intermediate stage
The length of the intermediate training plan depends upon the sports calendar, from which the coach selects a particular competition date. The training period can then be fixed, but its range will be from 10 to 12 weeks. This period should be divided into the following phases: (1) preparatory period, and (2) competitive period. Assuming a 10-week build-up prior to the selected competition, training will be divided into three blocks: weeks 1–4, weeks 5–8 and weeks 9–12.

Preparatory period (weeks 1–4)
The lifter now trains four times a week. Special attention should be paid to the development of fitness, including specialised strengthening and technique. Whilst the tonnage will be high, the intensity will be low. The training/recovery cycle is managed by alternating heavy and light training weeks. Thus week 1 is a light week, week 2 – heavy, week 3 – light, week 4 – heavy.

Top table: Stage 1; bottom table: Stage 2

DAY 1	DAY 2	DAY 3	DAY 4
Snatch	Snatch balance (behind neck)	Snatch balance (behind neck)	Clean
Power clean	Snatch pulls	Power clean	Power snatch
Clean pulls	Front squats	Clean pulls	Snatch pull
Jerk from racks	Dumb-bell press	Jerk from rack	Front squats
Back squat	Hyper-extensions	Back squat	Press behind neck
Sit-ups		Sit-ups	Hyper-extensions

Weeks 1–4

However, there is definite progression. For example, in week 4 the lifter is aiming to get a best ever 5 repetitions on most lifts. In the case of a lifter whose best snatch is 60kg, he would start week 1 with a top set for 5 repetitions at about 70%, i.e. 42.5kg; week 2 would be at 47.5kg, week 3 would be down to 45kg, and week 4 would be up to 50kg (approximately 80%), hopefully for a new best for 5 repetitions.

During weeks 1–4 all exercises will be done in 5 sets of 5 repetitions (with the exception of hyper-extensions and abdominal exercises which will be done 3 × 10 throughout). All sets are performed with progressively heavier weights until the last set which is a 'drop down' set, i.e. the heaviest set is always the penultimate one.

An example of the schedule that might be applied in the preparatory period is shown

above. (N.B. the exercises listed are only suggestions and the coach may vary these according to his assessment of the lifter's strengths and weaknesses. Also, the order of the exercises may be changed, e.g. some lifters prefer to use squat assistance exercises before pulling assistance exercises, or if a lifter is a weak jerker he may put this exercise first in his schedule.)

Competitive period (weeks 5–10)

During weeks 5–6 the lifter uses 2 × 5 and 5 × 3 for all exercises, except for the abdominals and hyper-extensions. The following schedules are suggested, subject to coaches' variations (weeks 5–6).

Week 7 is one of medium work load (85% of best lifts). Week 8 is one of heavy work load (90% of best lifts for the top set, plus 5 or so singles of 100%). During week

DAY 1	DAY 2	DAY 3	DAY 4
Snatch	Clean and jerk	Snatch	Clean and jerk
Power clean	Snatch balance	Power clean	Snatch balance
Clean pulls	Snatch pulls	Clean pulls	Snatch pulls
Jerk from racks	Back squat	Push press (behind neck)	Press behind neck
Front/Split squats	Hyper-extensions	Front/split squats	Hyper-extensions
Sit-ups		Sit-ups	

In a normal week on this schedule it is suggested that the lifter trains on two days, rests for one, trains on two and rests for two days. However, this may not be possible for all. Weeks 5–6.

9 the lifter trains up to starting weights, or 10kg below. Week 9 is a tapering off week: workouts should only last between 45 minutes and 1 hour so that energy reserves are built up. During these final weeks the lifter should get sufficient sleep and adequate nutrition, and he should practise good living habits.

The schedule for weeks 7–8 is as follows.

MEDIUM WEEK (7)	
Snatch and	2 × 3
Clean and jerk	5 × 2
Snatch balance	2 × 3
	3 × 2
Press behind neck	2 × 5
	3 × 3
Power snatch	3 × 3
Power clean)	3 × 2
Push press behind) neck	

HEAVY WEEK (8)	
Snatch and	2 × 3
Clean and jerk	2 × 2
	5 singles
Snatch balance	1 × 3
	2 × 2
	3 singles
Press behind neck	2 × 5
	3 × 3
Power snatch	3 × 3
Power clean)	3 × 2
Push press behind) neck	

All exercises, with the exception of pulls, should be 3 × 3 and then 5 singles, working up on the lifts to intended starting poundage or at least 10kg below. Pulls should be 3 × 3 followed by 5 × 2.

The final week is an effective tapering off up to the competition day. Gains in strength can hardly be expected during this period and all lifts should form a pattern of 'successful rehearsal', building confidence and a positive approach towards the forthcoming competition. Rest and relaxation are important requirements. Daily bodyweight checks should be made. The importance of the day of the competition demands that the lifter should not be distracted. He should check all personal kit, arrive early at the weigh-in, and ensure he has access to high energy foods which are easily digested.

Lifters who have successfully completed the novice and intermediate training programmes will now be suitably prepared for more rigorous loads and plans as employed by lifters of advanced qualification. See charts on pages 42 and 43.

Training lifters of advanced qualification

As one of the principle aims of training is to show continuously improving results, it is essential that those qualities of which we have already spoken should be fully developed. It will take time, possibly many years, and bearing this in mind it is essential that careful planning is undertaken by the coach or lifter.

During week 9 the following schedule is used:

MONDAY	TUESDAY	THURSDAY	FRIDAY
Snatch	Clean and jerk	Power snatch	Snatch
Snatch pulls	Clean pulls	Power clean	Clean and jerk
Front/split squats	Back squats	Front split squats	
Hyper-extensions	Hyper-extensions		

Training for lifters of 1st class standard

SCHEDULE 'A'	70%–80%	80%–90%	90%–100%
1 Snatch	1st month	2nd month	3rd month
	Kg reps	Kg reps	Kg reps
	55 × 5	65 × 3	70 × 3
	65 × 5	75 × 3	82½ × 3
	75 × 5	87½ × 3	90 × 3
	60 × 5	70 × 3	75 × 3
2 High pull Clean grip			
	85 × 5	90 × 5	100 × 5
	90 × 5	100 × 5	110 × 5
	100 × 5	110 × 5	120 × 5
	90 × 5	100 × 5	110 × 5
3 Jerk bal.			
	85 × 3	90 × 2	100 × 2
	90 × 3	100 × 2	110 × 2
	100 × 3	110 × 2	120 × 2
	90 × 3	95 × 2	110 × 2
4 Knee bends (Front or Split squats)		all for sets of 5 reps	
all for sets of			
	100	105	110 light
	110	115	120 medium
	120	125	130 heavy
5 Trunk fwd Bend (Good morning)			
	10 repetitions	light	
	10 repetitions	medium	
	10 repetitions	heavy	

Whilst the % levels for the training maximums will remain the same, the new all-out lift maximums at the end of each third month will give new working figures. Ideally, this plan should be worked for a period of nine months, so that by using the build-up/cut back principle progress should be maintained.

Planning falls into two categories: that of a long term nature and that of a short term nature. Short term plans will be 'run ups' to major competitions and as such are part of the long term plan. Within the plan detailed, realistic analysis of all goals to be achieved must be considered. This involves consideration of the sports calendar, preparation of individual sessions and organisation of the week's training and month by month group cycles. Together these make up the final plan, whether it is for a unit of 6, 9 or 12 months. These cycles, within the plan, will have different emphasis according to their time relationship and to principle competitions, and they may be selected for the development of skill and technique, powerbuilding, fitness, etc.

Group planning can be employed, but for most advanced lifters plans are individually prepared. Such plans will, however, have the same ingredients as those for the group, although it will be likely that additional technical work, supplementary exercises and varied overload and volume will be included. Generally speaking, the advanced lifter should train all the year round and this training can be broken down into two main cycles planned for two major competitions. There should be intermediate competitions, as results in these will be used in determining the load for the forthcoming

SCHEDULE 'B'	70%–80%	80%–90%	90%–100%
	1st month	2nd month	3rd month
	Kg reps	*Kg reps*	*Kg reps*
1 Clean and jerk Jerk last rep.			
	85 × 3	90 × 2	100 × 2
	90 × 3	100 × 2	110 × 2
	100 × 3	110 × 2	120 × 2
	90 × 3	95 × 2	110 × 2
2 High pull Snatch grip			
	50 × 5	60 × 5	70 × 5
	60 × 5	70 × 5	80 × 5
	70 × 5	80 × 5	90 × 5
	60 × 5	70 × 5	80 × 5
3 Snatch balance Squat or split			
	70 × 3	75 × 3	80 × 3
	80 × 3	85 × 3	90 × 3
	90 × 3	95 × 3	100 × 3
	75 × 3	80 × 3	90 × 3
4 Power snatch			
	50 × 3	55 × 3	60 × 3
	55 × 3	60 × 3	65 × 3
	60 × 3	65 × 3	70 × 3
	50 × 3	60 × 3	65 × 3
5 Upward jumps			
		5 repetitions	light
		5 repetitions	medium
		5 repetitions	heavy
6 Abdominals			
	5–10kg	5 repetitions	
		5 repetitions	
		5 repetitions	
		5 repetitions	
		5 repetitions	

Both 'A' and 'B' Schedules should be followed by a short period of fitness work:
after 'A' – standing long and high Jumps, short sprints;
after 'B' – 10 minutes relaxed jog trotting.

Alternate day schedule (A–B system) for lifters of first-class standard, in this case for men capable of 90kg snatch – 117.5kg jerk.

cycle. They will also help to show up both technical weaknesses and weaknesses in the previously completed training cycle.

Lifters should compete 5 to 6 times per year, with two of these being competitions in which the lifter hopes to achieve the highest results. At intermediate competi-tions the lifter should still aim for personal 'bests', as these will be the essential steps of progress and confidence reinforcement.

Each major competition for which a lifter and coach plan must have a training cycle based on the following periods: prepara-tory, competitive and transitional.

Preparatory period

The length of this period will depend upon the qualification of the lifter; indeed, for those in the novice category all their training may be dealt with under this heading. Much consideration should be given to the development of fitness, speed, co-ordination and endurance in the early stages. The advanced lifter will spend most of his time on the assistance exercises, and little time will be devoted to the classical lifts. Towards the end of this period, however, more attention will be spent on the snatch and the clean and jerk.

Competitive period

During the competitive period greater attention is paid to the classical lifts and those assistance exercises closely related to them. Maximum weights, within the range 90% to 100%, are used more frequently and certain exercises are advanced to the 110% range. During the last 30 to 20 days before competition those exercises which are slow and use maximum weights are generally reduced or excluded. The emphasis should be placed on power, so weights in the region of 90% + − are best used. Only a few of the most advanced lifters apply maximums in pulls and squats during the last 14 to 7 days and then with some five or six single repetitions only. During this period energy expenditure should not be high.

Transitional period

The transitional period is, in fact, a link between the competitive phase and a new preparatory period to be followed and should provide the lifter with a period of active rest. It should be arranged so that whilst the volume and intensity of the load are decreased and the number of training sessions in the week's cycle is cut down, the essential high levels of physical fitness are maintained and improved. This period can last up to 4 weeks.

It is essential to remember in all planning that an organism cannot maintain a steady, high level for a long period and that its efficiency tends to rise and fall. This must be taken into consideration when preparing all work cycles. The volume and intensity of the load must be varied, providing weeks of maximum, large, medium and light load and, indeed, within each week similar loading for each training session. Many of those lifters who enjoy ideal training conditions are able to train twice a day, morning and afternoon. Their work load is very high and they are placed in situations of great physical stress. Such people have very high levels of physical fitness and recuperative powers and their tolerance of the stressful situation is very well developed. Such work requires careful medical supervision at all stages.

The following is a long term plan which has been prepared for lifters of the highest qualification. It gives a build-up to two major competitions and whilst it is prepared on a group basis, i.e. for all lifters of the National 'A' Squad, coaches and lifters are advised to make individual changes where they consider them to be necessary.

Training programme for national squad lifters

The 12 weeks will be split up into 3 blocks: weeks 1–4, weeks 5–10 and weeks 11–12. During weeks 1–4 and 5–10 the same basic schedule will be followed, but during weeks 1–4 all exercises will be done as 5 sets of 5 repetitions, with the exception of hyper-extensions which will be 3 sets of 10 repetitions throughout. During weeks 5–10 all exercises are performed as 3 sets of 5 repetitions, then 5 sets of 3 repetitions, hyper-extensions excluded. All sets are performed with a progressively heavier weight until the last set which is a 'drop down set', i.e. the heaviest set is always the penultimate one.

A system of heavy and light weeks is used alternately, i.e. week 1 is light, week 2 is

DAY 1	DAY 2	DAY 3	DAY 4
Snatch	Snatch balance (behind neck)	Snatch balance (in front of neck)	Clean
Power clean	Power snatch	Power clean	Power snatch
Clean pulls	Snatch pull	Clean pull	Snatch pull
Jerk from rack	Front squat	Jerk from rack	Front squat
Back squat	Press behind neck	Back squat	Press behind neck
	Hyper-extensions		Hyper-extensions

Schedule for the lifter who trains 4 times per week

heavy, week 3 is light, week 4 is heavy, and so on. However, there is a definite progression, e.g. in week 4 the lifter is aiming to get a best ever for 5 repetitions on most lifts. Let us consider the snatch as an illustration; for a single we will say the lifter's record is 100kg. He would start week 1 with a top set for 5 repetitions at about 70%, i.e. 70kg. Week 2 would be up to 75kg, week 3 down to 72.5kg and then week 4 up to 80kg (approx. 80%) for a new best for 5.

This progression of heavy and light weeks carries on for weeks 5–10, but the repetitions change, as mentioned, and 3 repetition bests are worked on, aiming for about 90% for 3 in week 9.

It is considered that for national calibre lifters 4 workouts per week are the absolute minimum for progress and that 5 are better.

(Some lifters will work 6.) With this in mind, two separate schedules have been worked out to cater for lifters who train 4 times per week or 5 times per week. The exercises listed are suggestions and others may be put in at the discretion of the lifter and his coach, perhaps to cater for individual weaknesses. Also, the order of the exercises may be changed, e.g. if a lifter is a weak jerker he may put the jerk exercise first (see table above).

During a normal week on this schedule it is suggested that, ideally, the lifter trains for 2 days, rests for one, trains for two and rests for two. However, this may not be possible for all (see table below).

It is suggested that the lifter trains for 5 days in a row, or trains for 3, rests for 1, trains for 2, and rests for 1. After this

DAY 1	DAY 2	DAY 3	DAY 4	DAY 5
Snatch balance (behind neck)	Power clean	Snatch	Snatch balance (in front of neck)	Power clean
Power snatch	Clean pull	Clean	Power snatch	Clean pull
Snatch pull	Jerk from rack	Snatch pulls	Snatch pull	Jerk from rack
Front squat	Back squat	Clean pulls	Front squat	Back squat
Press behind neck	Hyper-extensions		Press behind neck	Hyper-extensions

Schedule for the lifter who trains 5 times per week

WEEK 11

Monday	Tuesday	Thursday	Friday
Snatch	Clean and jerk	Power snatch	Snatch
Snatch pull	Clean pull	Power clean	Clean and jerk
Front squat	Back squat	Squat	
Hyper-extensions	Hyper-extensions		

WEEK 12

Monday and Tuesday as Week 11		Wednesday	
		Power snatch 3 × 3 reps 3 × 2 reps	
		Power clean and jerk	
		Same sets and repetitions as for power snatch	

Schedule for the two weeks before the competition

10-week programme, the last 2 weeks prior to the championship should go as follows: all exercises, with the exception of pulls, should be 3 sets of 3 repetitions, then 5 sets of 1 repetition. The lifter should work up in the lifts to the intended starting attempts or at least 10kg below. Pulls should be 3 sets of 3 repetitions followed by 5 sets of 2 repetitions.

After the championship, several days' active rest should be followed by light training. Then, for the succeeding 9 weeks, a programme of 3 weekly cycles of light, medium and heavy weeks should begin. As far as exercises are concerned, the lifter trains on the original 4/5 days per week programme he used in weeks 1–10 prior to the championship. However, he will now substitute an extra snatch and clean exercise instead of a power clean and a power snatch, i.e. he will clean and snatch twice a week and power snatch and power clean once a week. He should clean *and* jerk in one of these.

All pulls should now be done as 8 sets of 3 repetitions. Squats should be done as 3 sets of 5 repetitions followed by 5 sets of 3 repetitions. The breakdown of sets and repetitions for the light, medium and heavy weeks is as follows for all other exercises:

LIGHT	MEDIUM	HEAVY
Snatch and clean jerk		
5 sets 3 reps	2 sets 3 reps 8 sets 2 reps	2 sets 3 reps 2 sets 2 reps 8 sets 1 rep
Snatch and balance		
5 sets 3 reps	5 sets 3 reps	5 sets 3 reps
Press behind neck		
3 sets 5 reps 3 sets 3 reps	3 sets 5 reps 3 sets 3 reps	3 sets 5 reps 3 sets 3 reps
Power snatch and power clean		
5 sets 3 reps	3 sets 3 reps 3 sets 2 reps	3 sets 3 reps 3 sets 2 reps

At the end of the ninth week, i.e. 3 cycles of the above, the lifter uses the same programme as he did for the two weeks prior to the championship.

Following this, lifters should take a period of active rest from lifting. However, it does not mean there should be no training at all. On the contrary, this time should be spent on fitness training so that the lifter can try to increase his cardio-vascular respiratory fitness. The type of work done will depend on the equipment and facilities available, but it must be of a progressive nature, e.g. repetition 60m sprints, circuit training, non-body contact ball games. Workouts should be recorded in the normal way.

Following this period, which may include some general weight training towards the end, another programme similar to the previous build-up will be planned.

Lifters should not be afraid to compete in matches during various stages of their programme and these should be treated as gauges of progress in the production of the desired totals at the major matches.

Training records must be kept at all times, either in a notebook or by using work sheets. These sheets show the exercises to be performed, the maximum weights to be used and the sets and repetitions to be attempted. See chart 1A on page 50.

Planning a programme

The preparation of schedules and training plans should not be approached haphazardly. The coach and the lifter should look forward to the most important competition for which the lifter will be trained. This means that a study of what is termed 'the sporting calendar' should be made. The most experienced lifters and those of national standard may well set their sights on competitions of the highest level, such as world and Olympic games, but for those of lesser qualification it would be more realistic to plan for good results at national or even divisional championship standard. Whilst the lifter should be ambitious in his

projection, he must also be realistic, and it is the duty of the coach to guide the lifter to climb a successful ladder of realistic achievements.

Once it has been decided which is to be the main competition, the coach should then work backwards from that day, looking carefully at all the dates of intermediate competitions, and should assess the value of such competitions. For example, it may be necessary at one or more of these stages to achieve a good result to qualify for the ultimate planned championship.

In addition, each of the intermediate competitions can be used as an indication of the lifter's progress and the best results that may be achieved at such competitions can be planned for and also used as a guide in the development of overload in the schedules and plans that are being prepared. This type of approach is called long term planning and it is essential that this overall view is kept in mind at all times. Within the long term plan, arrangements for intermediate competitions are worked out on a short term basis. It has been found that short term plans, generally, are most effective for periods of 10 to 12 weeks, concluding with a competition.

For very advanced lifters longer training periods can be attempted, but a pattern of fatigue may develop and the danger of injury through over-use may present itself. The shorter plans are divided into two phases. Phase 1 is called the preparation phase and phase 2 is named the competition phase.

Preparation phase

During this period there is a build-up of both quantity and quality of loading. The athlete is expected to take large work blocks, employing comparatively high repetitions. This generally requires that the exercises are performed on a 5 sets of 5 repetitions basis. The objectives of this type of work are to develop high levels of power and endurance, and it is very important for the coach to make certain that any technical errors that may exist are corrected. The period also helps to develop weightlifting fitness and it is essential in the development of rapid recovery from one heavy loading to the next. It generally lasts from 4 to 6 weeks.

Competition phase

During this phase far greater attention is paid to the classical lifts and to those assistance exercises which are very closely related to them. In many ways it could be considered a rehearsal in preparation for the competition to come. The overall quantity of work is generally reduced, whilst the quality is improved, i.e. maximum weights within the range 90%–100% are used on a regular basis. Certain exercises, especially the snatch and clean and jerk, can be advanced to the 100% + range. This may result in new best lifts and means that the lifter is forced to come to terms with the stressful elements that will be experienced in the competition. This has been regarded as a very important part of a lifter's development.

The last period of this phase is truly a period of rehearsal for competition, both in terms of weightlifting and of technical excellence. It is very important to emphasise that now is a time for success and the development of determination and psychological strength. There should be as little failure on any attempts as possible. In this way the lifter builds up energy reserves and a strong belief in his abilities for the competition to come.

The last three weeks in particular are critical to the lifter. He must build up to a peak on the day of competition, making certain that he has not come 'to the boil' too soon. For the majority of lifters the very heaviest weights, i.e. those that they hope to lift in competition, are generally not attempted during the last seven days. During the last week the lifter tapers off to the competition day, making certain that all training is technically sound and so designed as to build energy stores. The general advice is that the lifter should take one or two days' rest prior to the competition. However, the more advanced lifters find that it is preferable to train with very light weights right up until the day of com-

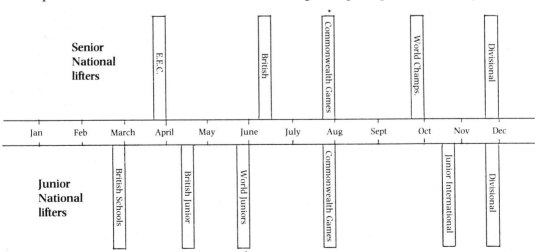

* Competitions selected as most important. (Some Junior lifters of special ability may well be selected for Commonwealth Games or Senior World Championships.)

Chart 2 World Training Plan

PREPARATION PERIOD – 5 WEEKS

	WEEK 1	WEEK 2	WEEK 3	WEEK 4		WEEK 5	
Sets and reps	5 × 5	5 × 5	5 × 5	4 × 3	4 × 3	3 × 5	5 × 3
% of best lifts	70	80	75	80	85	80	90
All back squats 5 sets of 3 at:	70%	80%	75%	85%		90%	

COMPETITION PERIOD

	WEEK 6	WEEK 7	WEEK 8	
Sets and reps	5 × 3 3 × 2 and 5 singles	5 × 3 3 × 2	5 × 3 3 × 2 and 5 singles	
% top set singles to	85 97.5	82.5	90 100+	
All back squats	5 × 2 95%	5 × 3 85%	2 × 2 2 × 2 3 singles	90% 95% 100+%

TAPERING DOWN

WEEK 9

Olympic lifts to starting kg.
Other lifts in the range to 95%

Technique correct
Bodyweight control

WEEK 10

Olympic lifts
Snatch 10kg below starting kg
Clean and jerk (light)
Other lifts (light and fast)

Technique correct
Bodyweight control

Layout of 10-week training plan

petition. Since most lifters of advanced qualification train twice every day, it is quite acceptable that they should do this.

Any programmes that are subsequently devised should be based upon these considerations. It is up to the coach to work out suitable schedules for his lifters. The schedules and plans which are shown in this book are examples only, because there is no magic schedule which will produce champions every time. Coaches must also be aware of any particular weaknesses or individual problems that lifters may have and must try to overcome them in the plans of the training programmes that they devise.

Long term training plans

On p. 48 is a typical plan showing the build-up to a major competition, including intermediate competitions of an important nature which can be considered for qualification and as progress incentives.

The coach should devise a similar plan, remembering that the dates of such competitions are chosen by other organisations and so are not under his control. He must, therefore, be prepared to organise and plan with the calendar of competitions in mind.

30-week plan for a world championship

This relates to the 10-week training programme as laid out under Item WTP (World Training Plan). See charts 2A and 2B.

Schedules are based on preparation and competition periods. Schedules A and B are of a power development nature and Schedules C and D relate very much more

Chart 1A

	DAY 1						DAY 2						DAY 3					DAY 4					

WEEK 1

Exercise	3	2	8	5	10	
Max kg						
Sets and reps	5×5	5×5	5×5	5×5	5×5

DAY 2 — Exercise: 13a/14, 1, 7, 9, 11, 12 — Sets and reps: 5×5, 5×5, 5×5, 5×5, 5×5, 3×10
DAY 3 — Exercise: 13/14, 2, 8, 5, 10 — Sets and reps: 5×5, 5×5, 5×5, 5×5, 5×5
DAY 4 — Exercise: 4, 1, 7, 9, 11, 12 — Sets and reps: 5×5, 5×5, 5×5, 5×5, 5×5, 3×10

WEEK 2

DAY 1 — Exercise: 3, 2, 8, 5, 10 — Sets and reps: 5×5, 5×5, 5×5, 5×5, 5×5
DAY 2 — Exercise: 13a/14, 1, 7, 9, 11, 12 — Sets and reps: 5×5, 5×5, 5×5, 5×5, 5×5, 3×10
DAY 3 — Exercise: 13/14, 2, 8, 5, 10 — Sets and reps: 5×5, 5×5, 5×5, 5×5, 5×5
DAY 4 — Exercise: 4, 1, 7, 9, 11, 12 — Sets and reps: 5×5, 5×5, 5×5, 5×5, 5×5, 3×10

WEEK 3

DAY 1 — Exercise: 3, 2, 8, 5, 10 — Sets and reps: 5×5, 5×5, 5×5, 5×5, 5×5
DAY 2 — Exercise: 13a/14, 1, 7, 9, 11, 12 — Sets and reps: 5×5, 5×5, 5×5, 5×5, 5×5, 3×10
DAY 3 — Exercise: 13/14, 2, 8, 5, 10 — Sets and reps: 5×5, 5×5, 5×5, 5×5, 5×5
DAY 4 — Exercise: 4, 1, 7, 9, 11, 12 — Sets and reps: 5×5, 5×5, 5×5, 5×5, 5×5, 3×10

WEEK 4

DAY 1 — Exercise: 3, 2, 8, 5, 10 — Sets and reps: 5×5, 5×5, 5×5, 5×5, 5×5
DAY 2 — Exercise: 13a/14, 1, 7, 9, 11, 12 — Sets and reps: 5×5, 5×5, 5×5, 5×5, 5×5, 3×10
DAY 3 — Exercise: 13/14, 2, 8, 5, 10 — Sets and reps: 5×5, 5×5, 5×5, 5×5, 5×5
DAY 4 — Exercise: 4, 1, 7, 9, 11, 12 — Sets and reps: 5×5, 5×5, 5×5, 5×5, 5×5, 3×10

WEEK 5

DAY 1 — Exercise: 3, 2, 8, 5, 10 — Sets and reps: 3×5/5×3, 3×5/5×3, 3×5/5×3, 3×5/5×3, 5×5
DAY 2 — Exercise: 13a/14, 1, 7, 9, 11, 12 — Sets and reps: 3×5/5×3, 3×5/5×3, 3×5/5×3, 5×5, 3×5/5×3, 3×10
DAY 3 — Exercise: 13/14, 2, 8, 5, 10 — Sets and reps: 3×5/5×3, 3×5/5×3, 3×5/5×3, 3×5/5×3, 5×5
DAY 4 — Exercise: 4, 1, 7, 9, 11, 12 — Sets and reps: 3×5/5×3, 3×5/5×3, 3×5/5×3, 5×5, 3×5/5×3, 3×10

WEEK 6

DAY 1 — Exercise: 3, 2, 8, 5, 10 — Sets and reps: 3×5/5×3, 3×5/5×3, 3×5/5×3, 3×5/5×3, 5×5
DAY 2 — Exercise: 13a/14, 1, 7, 9, 11, 12 — Sets and reps: 3×5/5×3, 3×5/5×3, 3×5/5×3, 5×5, 3×5/5×3, 3×10
DAY 3 — Exercise: 13/14, 2, 8, 5, 10 — Sets and reps: 3×5/5×3, 3×5/5×3, 3×5/5×3, 3×5/5×3, 5×5
DAY 4 — Exercise: 4, 1, 7, 9, 11, 12 — Sets and reps: 3×5/5×3, 3×5/5×3, 3×5/5×3, 5×5, 3×5/5×3, 3×10

WEEK 7

DAY 1 — Exercise: 3, 2, 8, 5, 10 — Sets and reps: 3×5/5×3, 3×5/5×3, 3×5/5×3, 3×5/5×3, 5×5
DAY 2 — Exercise: 13a/14, 1, 7, 9, 11, 12 — Sets and reps: 3×5/5×3, 3×5/5×3, 3×5/5×3, 5×5, 3×5/5×3, 3×10
DAY 3 — Exercise: 13/14, 2, 8, 5, 10 — Sets and reps: 3×5/5×3, 3×5/5×3, 3×5/5×3, 3×5/5×3, 5×5
DAY 4 — Exercise: 4, 1, 7, 9, 11, 12 — Sets and reps: 3×5/5×3, 3×5/5×3, 3×5/5×3, 5×5, 3×5/5×3, 3×10

WEEK 8

DAY 1 — Exercise: 3, 2, 8, 5, 10 — Sets and reps: 3×5/5×3, 3×5/5×3, 3×5/5×3, 3×5/5×3, 5×5
DAY 2 — Exercise: 13a/14, 1, 7, 9, 11, 12 — Sets and reps: 3×5/5×3, 3×5/5×3, 3×5/5×3, 5×5, 3×5/5×3, 3×10
DAY 3 — Exercise: 13/14, 2, 8, 5, 10 — Sets and reps: 3×5/5×3, 3×5/5×3, 3×5/5×3, 3×5/5×3, 5×5
DAY 4 — Exercise: 4, 1, 7, 9, 11, 12 — Sets and reps: 3×5/5×3, 3×5/5×3, 3×5/5×3, 5×5, 3×5/5×3, 3×10

WEEK 9

DAY 1 — Exercise: 3, 2, 8, 5, 10 — Sets and reps: 3×5/5×3, 3×5/5×3, 3×5/5×3, 3×5/5×3, 5×5
DAY 2 — Exercise: 13a/14, 1, 7, 9, 11, 12 — Sets and reps: 3×5/5×3, 3×5/5×3, 3×5/5×3, 5×5, 3×5/5×3, 3×10
DAY 3 — Exercise: 13/14, 2, 8, 5, 10 — Sets and reps: 3×5/5×3, 3×5/5×3, 3×5/5×3, 3×5/5×3, 5×5
DAY 4 — Exercise: 4, 1, 7, 9, 11, 12 — Sets and reps: 3×5/5×3, 3×5/5×3, 3×5/5×3, 5×5, 3×5/5×3, 3×10

WEEK 10

DAY 1 — Exercise: 3, 2, 8, 5, 10 — Sets and reps: 3×5/5×3, 3×5/5×3, 3×5/5×3, 3×5/5×3, 5×5
DAY 2 — Exercise: 13a/14, 1, 7, 9, 11, 12 — Sets and reps: 3×5/5×3, 3×5/5×3, 3×5/5×3, 5×5, 3×5/5×3, 3×10
DAY 3 — Exercise: 13/14, 2, 8, 5, 10 — Sets and reps: 3×5/5×3, 3×5/5×3, 3×5/5×3, 3×5/5×3, 5×5
DAY 4 — Exercise: 4, 1, 7, 9, 11, 12 — Sets and reps: 3×5/5×3, 3×5/5×3, 3×5/5×3, 5×5, 3×5/5×3, 3×10

Continued on page 51

12 week 4 days per week training programme

	DAY 1				DAY 2				DAY 3				DAY 4		
WEEK 11															
Exercise	**3**	7	9	12	**6**	8	10	12	**1**	2	9	12	**3**	6	12
Max kg															
Sets and reps	**3×3**	3×3	3×3	3×10	**3×3**	3×3			**3×3**	3×3	3×3		**3×5**	3×5	3×10
	6×1	5×2	6×1		**6×1**	5×2	5×3	3×10	**3×2**	5×2	6×1	3×10	**5×3**	5×3	
WEEK 12															
Exercise	**3**	7	9	12	**6**	8	10	12	**1**	2			REST FOR 2 DAYS PRIOR TO COMP.		
Max kg															
Sets and reps	**3×3**	3×3	3×5	3×10	**3×3**	3×5			**3×3**	3×3					
	6×1	5×2	6×1		**6×1**	5×2	5×3	3×10	**3×2**	3×2					

1 Power snatch
2 Power clean
3 Snatch
4 Clean
5 Jerk from racks
6 Clean & jerk
7 Snatch pull
8 Clean pull
9 Front or split squat
10 Back squat
11 Press behind neck
12 Hyper-extensions
13 Squat snatch bal. from front
13a Squat snatch bal. from back
14 Split snatch bal. from front

Chart 2A World Training Plan (W.T.P.)

SCHEDULE A	LOADING ZONE	CALENDAR WEEKS
Snatch balance	weeks 1 and 2	(01–02)
Power snatch	weeks 4 and 5	(03–04)
Clean pulls	weeks 1 and 2	(08–09)
Back squat	weeks 4 and 5	(10–11)
Barbell press	weeks 5 and 6	(15–16)
SCHEDULE B		
Jerk from stands	weeks 1 and 2	(21 and 22)
Power clean		
Snatch pulls	weeks 4 and 5	(23–24)
Front squat		
D/B press		
SCHEDULE C		
Snatch balance	weeks 6–7–8	(05–06–07)
Snatch		
Clean pulls	weeks 6–7–8	(12–13–14)
Back squat		
SCHEDULE D		
Clean and jerk	weeks 7–8–9–10	(17–18–19–20)
Snatch pulls	weeks 6–7–8–9–10	(25–26–27–28–29–30)
Front squat		

30 weeks to world championship; 20 weeks to national championship.

closely to the competition lifts. See chart 2A on page 51.

The loadings' zones are shown for preparation and competition phases. Week 3 loadings have been eliminated. This has been necessary in order to obtain a proper balance in the programme leading to the two championships, and also to increase the loading by reaching the more intense workouts more quickly. See Chart 2 on page 49.

Calendar weeks are the periods when each loading zone should be in operation.

In this example, the national championship takes place after 20 weeks. Since there is no competition after 10 weeks, as would be normal, the programme can be repeated from the eighth to the sixteenth week. This then leaves a final run to the national championship of four weeks. See pages 51 and 57.

Following the national championship, the team will be selected for the world championship. Training will commence immediately over a ten-week programme of four weeks of preparation period and six weeks of competition period leading to the day of competition. In this period the loading zone, week 6, is repeated, giving a second medium high intensity training. The effect is to sharpen the lifter and to develop extra power intensity.

Throughout the period a number of squad training meetings have been planned. These help to keep up team spirit and incentive and to help the coach monitor the progress of the lifters. Here they are placed at the end of blocks of training.

Examples of training cycles

WEEK 1	WEEK 2	WEEK 3	WEEK 4	
FOR LIFTERS OF 1st CLASS AND INTERMEDIATE QUALIFICATION			DAY 1	Medium heavy intensity. 1½ hours only
			DAY 2	
Light volume	Medium volume	Heavy intensity Low reps Heavy weights	DAY 3	Very light. 5kg below 1st attempt
			DAY 4	
FOR LIFTERS OF ADVANCED QUALIFICATION			DAY 5	R E S T
Medium volume	Heavy intensity Top set 90% Singles 100% +	Olympic lifts to first attempts Singles – 10kg below best result	DAY 6	Competition
			DAY 7	
Build up period. There should be no failure during this time			Final week	

Weekly breakdown of last month training cycle prior to competition

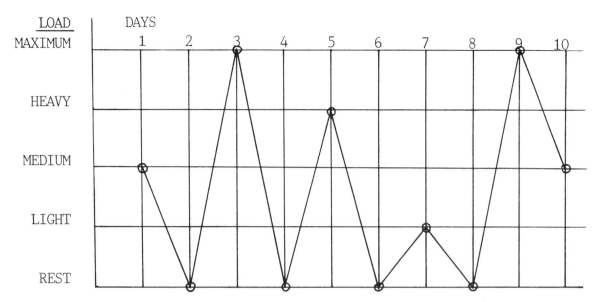

Distribution of loads for a nine-day training cycle. This plan provides for 2 maximum loads and 1 heavy load within a period of 9 training days. (**1st class qualification**.)

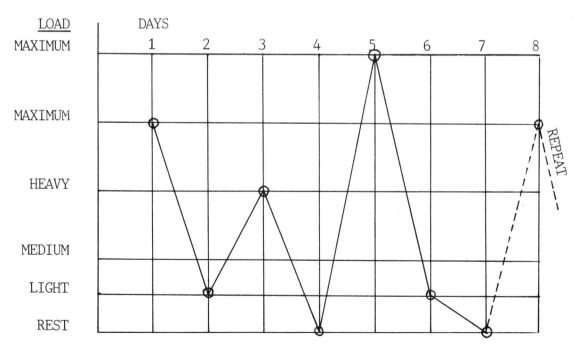

Distribution of loads for a seven-day training cycle. This plan provides for 1 maximum + load, 1 maximum load, and 1 heavy load within a period of 7 training days. (**Advanced qualification**.)

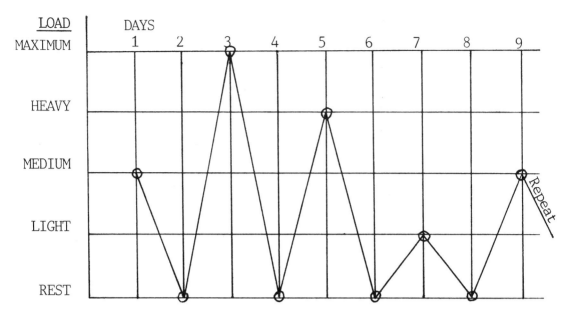

Distribution of loads for a nine-day training cycle. This plan provides for 1 maximum load and 1 heavy load within a period of 9 training days. (**Novice qualification**.)

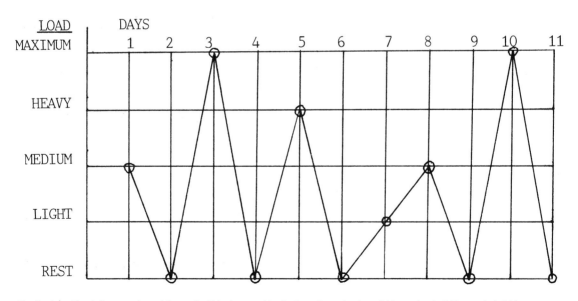

Distribution of loads for a ten-day training cycle. This plan provides for 2 maximum loads and 1 heavy load within a period of 10 training days. (**Intermediate qualification**)

Kg	60%	65%	70%	75%	80%	85%	90%	92.5%	95%	97.5%	102.5%	105%	107.5%	110%
75	45	48.7	52.5	56.2	60	63.7	67.5	69.3	71.2	73.1	76.8	78.7	80.6	82.5
77.5	46.5	50.3	54.2	58.1	62	65.8	69.7	71.6	73.6	75.5	79.4	81.3	83.3	85.2
80	48	52	56	60	64	68	72	74	76	78	82	84	86	88
82.5	49.5	53.6	57.7	61.8	66	70.1	74.2	76.2	78.3	80.4	84.5	86.6	88.6	90.7
85	51	55.2	59.5	63.7	68	72.2	76.5	78.6	87.0	82.8	87.1	89.2	91.3	93.5
87.5	52.5	56.8	61.2	65.6	70	74.3	78.7	80.9	83.1	85.3	89.6	91.8	94	96.2
90	54	58.5	63	67.5	72	76.5	81	83.2	85.5	87.7	92.2	94.5	96.7	99
92.5	55.5	60.1	64.7	69.3	74	78.6	83.2	85.5	87.8	90.1	94.8	97.1	99.4	101.7
95	57	61.7	66.5	71.2	76	80.7	85.5	87.8	90.2	92.6	97.3	99.7	102	104.4
97.5	58.5	63.3	68.2	73.1	78	82.8	87.7	90.1	92.6	95	99.9	102.3	104.8	107.2
100	60	65	70	75	80	85	90	92.5	95	97.5	102.5	105	107.5	110
102.5	61.5	66.6	71.7	76.8	82	87.1	92.2	94.8	97.3	99.9	105	107.6	110.1	112.7
105	63	68.2	73.5	78.7	84	89.2	94.5	97.1	99.7	102.3	107.6	110.2	112.8	115.5
107.5	64.5	69.8	75.2	80.6	86	91.3	96.7	99.4	102.1	104.8	110.1	112.8	115.5	118.2
110	66	71.5	77	82.5	88	93.5	99	101.7	104.5	107.2	112.7	115.5	118.2	121
112.5	67.5	73.1	78.1	84.3	90	95.6	101.2	104	106.8	109.6	115.3	118.1	120.9	123.7
115	69	74.7	80.5	86.2	92	97.7	103.5	106.3	109.2	112.1	117.8	120.7	123.6	126.5
117.5	70.5	76.3	82.2	88.1	94	99.8	105.7	108.6	111.6	114.5	120.4	123.3	126.3	129.2
120	72	78	84	90	96	102	108	110.9	114	117	123	126	129	132
122.5	73.5	79.6	85.7	91.8	98	104.1	110.2	113.3	116.3	119.4	125.5	128.6	131.6	134.7
125	75	81.2	87.5	93.7	100	106.2	112.5	115.6	118.7	121.8	128.1	131.2	134.3	137.4
127.5	76.5	82.8	89.2	95.6	102	108.3	114.7	117.9	121.1	124.3	130.6	133.8	137	140.2
130	78	84.5	91	97.5	104	110.5	117	120.2	123.5	126.7	133.2	136.5	139.7	143
132.5	79.5	86.1	92.7	99.3	106	112.6	119.2	122.5	125.8	129.1	135.8	139.1	142.4	145.7
135	81	87.7	94.5	101.2	108	114.7	121.5	124.8	128.2	131.6	138.3	141.7	145.1	148.5
137.5	82.5	89.3	96.2	103.1	110	116.8	123.7	127.1	130.6	134	140.9	144.3	147.8	151.2
140	84	91	98	105	112	119	126	129.4	133	136.5	143.5	147	150.5	154
142.5	85.5	92.6	99.7	106.8	114	121.1	128.2	131.8	135.2	138.9	146	149.6	153.1	156.7
145	87	94.2	101.5	108.7	116	123.2	130.5	134.1	137.7	141.3	148.6	152.2	155.8	159.5
147.5	88.5	95.8	103.2	110.6	118	125.3	132.7	136.4	140.1	143.8	151.1	154.8	158.5	162.2
150	90	97.5	105	112.5	120	127.5	135	138.7	142.5	146.2	153.7	157.5	161.2	165
152.5	91.5	99.1	106.7	114.3	122	129.6	137.2	141	144.8	148.6	156.2	160.1	163.8	167.7
155	93	100.7	108.5	116.2	124	131.7	139.5	143.3	147.2	151	158.8	162.7	166.5	170.5
157.5	94.5	102.3	110.2	118.1	126	133.8	141.7	145.6	149.6	153.5	161.3	165.3	169.2	173.2
160	96	104	112	120	128	136	144	147.9	152	155.9	163.9	168	171.9	176

TO17405

Kg	60%	65%	70%	75%	80%	85%	90%	92.5%	95%	97.5%	102.5%	105%	107.5%	110%
162.5	97.5	105.6	113.7	121.8	130	138.1	146.2	150.2	154.3	158.3	166.5	170.6	174.6	178.7
165	99	107.2	115.5	123.7	132	140.2	148.5	152.5	156.7	160.8	169	173.2	177.3	181.5
167.5	100.5	108.8	117.2	125.6	134	142.3	150.7	154.8	159.1	163.2	171.6	175.8	180	184.2
170	102	110.5	119	127.5	136	144.5	153	157.2	161.5	165.6	174.2	178.5	182.7	187
172.5	103.5	112.1	120.7	129.3	138	146.6	155.2	159.5	163.8	168.1	176.7	181.1	185.5	189.7
175	105	113.7	122.5	131.2	140	148.7	157.5	161.8	166.2	170.6	179.3	183.7	188.1	192.5
177.5	106	115.3	124.2	133.1	142	150.8	159.7	164.1	168.5	173	181.8	186.3	190.7	195.1
180	108	117	126	135	144	153	162	166.5	172	175.5	184.5	189	193.5	198
182.5	109.5	118.6	127.7	136.8	146	155.1	164.2	168.7	173.3	177.9	187	191.5	196.1	200.7
185	111	120.2	129.5	138.7	148	157.2	166.5	171.1	175.7	180.3	189.6	194.2	198.8	203.4
187.5	112.5	121.8	131.2	140.6	150	159.3	168.7	173.4	178	182.7	192.1	196.8	201.4	206.1
190	114	123.5	133	142.5	152	161.5	171	175.7	180.4	185.1	194.5	199.2	203.9	208.6
192.5	115.5	125.1	134.7	144.3	154	163.6	173.2	178	182.8	187.6	197.2	202	206.8	211.7
195	117	126.7	136.5	146.2	156	165.7	175.5	180.3	185.2	190.1	199.8	204.7	209.5	214.4
197.5	118.5	128.3	138.2	148.1	158	167.8	177.6	182.5	187.4	192.4	202.2	207.2	212.1	217
200	120	130	140	150	160	170	180	185	190	195	205	210	215	220
202.5	121.5	131.6	141.7	151.8	162	172.1	182.2	187.2	192.3	197.4	207.5	212.5	217.6	222.7
205	123	133.2	143.5	153.7	164.	174.2	184.5	189.6	194.7	199.8	210.1	215.2	220.3	225.4
207.5	124.5	134.5	145.2	155.6	166	176.3	186.7	191.9	197	202.2	212.6	217.8	222.9	228.1
210	126	136.5	147	157.5	168	178.5	189	194.2	199.5	204.7	215.2	220.5	225.7	231
212.5	127.5	138.1	148.7	159.3	170	180.6	191.2	196.5	201.8	207.1	217.7	223	228.3	233.7
215	129	139.7	150.5	161.2	172	182.7	193.5	198.8	204.2	209.6	220.3	225.7	231	236.4
217.5	130.5	141.3	152.2	163.1	174	184.8	195.7	201.1	206.5	212	222.8	228.3	233.7	239.1
220	132	143	154	165	176	187	198	203.5	209	214.5	225.5	231	236.5	242
222.5	133.5	144.6	155.7	166.8	178	189.1	200.2	205.7	211.3	216.9	228	233.5	239.1	244.7
225	135	146.2	157.5	168.7	180	191.2	202.5	208.1	213.7	219.3	230.6	236.2	241.8	247.4

These figures should be rounded up or down to the nearest 2.5 or 5kg weights.

Percentage table

Chart 2B World Training Plan

WEEK 1	A/B/A/B			
2	A/B/A/B			
3	A/B/A/B			
4	A/B/A/B		Squad	
5		C/D/C/D		
6		C/D/C/D		
7		C/D/C/D		
8	A/B/A/B			
9	A/B/A/B			
10	A/B/A/B			
11	A/B/A/B		Squad	
12		C/D/C/D		
13		C/D/C/D		
14		C/D/C/D	Squad	
15	A/B/A/B			
16	A/B/A/B			
17		C/D/C/D		
18		C/D/C/D		
19		C/D/C/D		
20		C/D/C/D		British champs
21	A/B/A/B			
22	A/B/A/B			
23	A/B/A/B			
24	A/B/A/B		Squad	
25		C/D/C/D		
26		C/D/C/D		
27		C/D/C/D	Squad	
28		C/D/C/D		
29		C/D/C/D		World champs
30		C/D/C/D		World champs
31				

POWERLIFTING

Modern powerlifting has developed from the original strength set lifting. This was evolved by the B.A.W.L.A. which selected a set of lifts to be used for competition by lifters involved with the olympic lifts.

The original lifts in the strength set were composed of the two-hand curl, the bench press and the squat. These lifts were selected for competition because they were most commonly used and of greatest importance in the training schedules and programmes of all forms of strength training, weight training and body building. In the early 1960s the curl was replaced by the two-hand dead lift. This insured a set of lifts which would demonstrate a lifter's basic strength to the fullest advantage. The order of performance of the lifts was also changed, making the squat the first lift and the dead lift the last of the three.

The bend press remained in the middle, giving the lifters a certain amount of respite between the two very heavy massive body movements.

Standards of technique and training methods have improved considerably since then and the modern powerlifter is a dedicated and determined athlete.

Competitions take place at national and international level and world championships are also held.

Study the text and photographs carefully, as these illustrate the basic fundamentals of the sport.

The squat

Starting position
The bar is taken from the stands to rest across the shoulders behind the neck and is held as low down as is possible whilst conforming to the rules of this lift. (See I.P.F. rulebook.)

The hands should grasp the barbell firmly, which will maintain the position of the bar on the shoulders throughout the lift, and should be spaced as is most comfortable for the lifter. (*See photograph 1.*)

The head is held up, eyes looking forwards and up, and the chest is lifted high. This will give a firm and positive position for the upper body and help to establish balance and a sense of determination.

The position of the feet is generally slightly wider than hip width, and the toes are turned out. The weight of the body and bar must rest evenly over all the surface of the foot. Some more experienced lifters find that a wider foot stance is of benefit to them, but the principle criterion in selecting the foot spacing is that the lifter should feel as comfortable as possible whilst gaining the full benefit of a strong and balanced starting position.

The movement
Taking a deep breath and maintaining a high chest, the lifter lowers the body by bending the legs to the position as shown in photograph 3. During this lowering there will be some inclination of the trunk forwards *see photograph 2*, but the back must be

The squat 1. Starting position

2. Lowering the bar

3. Maximum depth in the lift

kept straight and the lifter must fight against any tendency for the spine to round. The depth to which the body is lowered is controlled by the rules of the lift which state that the top surface of the legs at the hip joint should be lower than the top of the knees.

Training must ensure that the lifter learns to feel this position; since there is no signal from the referee to stand erect, the onus is on the lifter as to when to make his effort to rise.

All squatting should therefore be performed to at least the minimum position, as described above. Lifters are advised not to go into the very deepest full squat position.

Recovery
When the lifter is confident that he has reached the necessary low position, he must begin immediately his recovery. It is at this point, of course, that he will experience great difficulty and he will require great determination and fighting spirit to force himself back to the erect position. It is vitally important that the knees remain turned outwards. Often, due to the very strong adductor muscles that lie along the inside of the thigh, the knees are pulled inwards during recovery. This action tends to force the hips backwards, consequently tipping the chest forwards, placing the lifter in a very poor mechanical position, dissipating much of the leg drive and throwing too great a proportion of the resistance on the lower back. Great determination is required, therefore, in all training for this lift to make certain that the knees are kept turned outwards so that the hips are kept closer over the base and the chest is kept high.

Remember that during the recovery advantage can be gained by keeping the head held back and looking up. Think of driving strongly upwards with the head.

The bench press 1. Preparation for the lift

The bench press

Starting position

It is essential that the starting position is stable and balanced. (Make certain that the bench apparatus is of a very rigid and strong construction.) The lifter lies on the bench, with his buttocks, shoulders and head in contact with the bench. These body parts must remain in place throughout the lift. The knees are bent so that the feet can be placed flat on the floor. This position of the feet will greatly assist the stability of the lifter on the bench.

The major muscle which is employed during this lift, and especially at the start of the movement, is the pectoralis major. Since it is a fan-shaped muscle, many of its lower fibres pull the arm towards the side rather than lifting the upper arm in a more vertical pathway as is demanded when driving the bar from the chest. To get full advantage from the action of this large muscle, the body should be arched so that the sternum can be placed in a more vertical position. (*See photograph 1.*) In this way the lower fibres of the pectoralis major are able to pull more vertically. In photograph 1 the lifter is seen positioning himself in this arch prior to being handed the barbell. It is known as the Collins Arch named after Ron Collins (G.B.), many times world champion and world record holder.

Maintaining the position, as described above, the barbell is handed to the lifter. The bar should be gripped with a hand spacing that is as comfortable to the lifter as possible (whilst conforming to the I.P.F. rules). However, it is recommended that in order to obtain the best mechanical

Above 2. Starting position. **Below** 3. Mid-section of the bench press

4. Do not train on this lift alone

advantage the hands should be so spaced that when the bar is resting on the chest the forearms are near to the vertical position. It is recognised, of course, that there will be considerable variation with individual lifters and that best results will be achieved by experimentation and experience.

Lowering to starting position
The lifter takes a deep breath, stabilising the chest to give a firm base for the muscular action involved in the lift.

In his own time the lifter lowers the bar to his chest. This must be done under control. When the bar comes to rest on the chest and is quite still the lifter receives a signal from the referee to commence the press. (*See photograph 2.*) The lifter drives the bar from the chest with great fierceness. In the initial

starting position, when the bar is resting on the chest, it will not lie over the fulcrum of the shoulder joint but will be some 2 or 3 inches forward of this point. This means that there is a forward weight arm and consequent mechanical disadvantage right from the start of the drive. The forward weight arm must be eliminated and in order to do this the lifter eases the bar back during the drive to bring it over the shoulder fulcrum.

Whilst the drive must be very determined, care must be taken to ensure than the elbows are not lifted upwards and forwards, as this would throw too great a resistance on the triceps too soon. It will be in the mid-range of the movement that the lifter will encounter the greatest difficulties. This area is known as the 'sticking point' or point of the greatest mechanical and anatomical disadvantage. Here the horizontal weight arms are at their greatest and there is a weak link between the change over of one muscle group with another.

The initial part of the drive is developed by strong action of the pectoralis major, anterior deltoid and serratus anterior. At the mid-section of the press the role of these muscles is diminishing and the triceps are beginning to take on a greater responsibility in the movement. (*See photograph 3.*) It is here that the weakness occurs. This section of the lift is the true test of the lifter's character. As the bar passes through the mid-range, it becomes increasingly easy to complete the movement.

The lift is completed when the arms are fully straightened. (*See photograph 4.*) A signal will then be given by the referee to take the bar from the lifter.

It is important to note that throughout the lift the high arch is maintained.

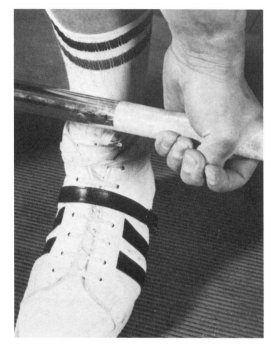

Above The two-hands dead lift 1. The hook grip. *Opposite page* 3. Starting position

2. The alternate gripping method

The two-hands dead lift

The two-hands dead lift is the king of the three power lifts, being the ultimate test of strength and fighting spirit. It is also the most important lift, since it is the last, and a good performance can make the difference between winning and losing.

The movement
In this lift the weight is taken from the ground to a final position; the legs are straight, the body is erect and the shoulders are braced back. At no time during the execution of the movement must the bar stop on its upward path.

One of the most important components controlling the successful completion of the lift is a strong grip. It is recommended that the lifter employs the method known as 'hooking'. The hook grip is performed by placing the top segment of the thumb along the barbell and wrapping the first and second finger around it, thereby squeezing it against the bar. (*See photograph 1*.) Additional difficulties with the grip occur due to the bending of the bar as the weight is lifted from the floor. The bend or spring causes the bar to roll in the hands and it is this rolling action that can break the grip. The lifter is therefore advised to use the alternate gripping method in which one hand faces forwards and the other faces backwards. (*See photograph 2*.) The bar will then be unable to roll and so the grip remains secure.

The starting position
The feet are placed underneath the bar, approximately hip width apart. It is important that the lifter feels all his weight evenly over his feet. Bending the knees and flexing his hips, he lowers his body and grips the bar.

It is recommended that the width of grip should be slightly wider than shoulder width, with the arms outside the knees. The back is flat and strongly braced and the shoulders are slightly in advance of the line of the bar.

The starting position must be well balanced and positive in approach. (*See photograph 3*.)

4. The back should be kept as flat as possible

5. Approach the lift with determination

The lift

Because of the forward inclination of the shins, the bar will be over the junction of the main body of the foot and the toes will be towards the front of the base. If the bar was lifted vertically from this position, the tendency would be for the lifter to be pulled forwards off balance. If the lifter loses balance, he is unable to use maximum force. It is essential that during the first phase of the lift from floor to knee height the bar should be eased back inwards towards the shins, so that by the time it reaches the height of the knees it is central over the base. It is possible to do this because the first part of the lift is initiated by a strong straightening of the legs; by the time the bar has reached knee height the shins have reached a vertical position and the knees have moved back. Throughout this strong leg drive the lifter should fight to keep his back strong and flat.

There will be a tendency for the back to be pulled into a rounded position, but this should be resisted. The angle of the back should be maintained from the starting position, lifting the hips and the shoulders simultaneously. (*See photograph 4.*)

Photograph 4 illustrates the middle range of the movement and it is here that the lifter is likely to experience greatest difficulty. At this point the distance between the active fulcrum of the hips and a vertical line through the bar results in a long weight arm and a position of mechanical disadvantage. In addition, there is an anatomical takeover from the muscles which extend the knee, quadriceps femoris, to those which extend the hip, gluteal and hamstring muscles. This results in anatomical disadvantage. Very great determination must be employed to get through this difficult range.

As the bar passes the knees and the lower part of the thigh great resistance will be placed upon the extensors of the hip and the muscles of the back. The hip muscles, especially, work very strongly to pull the body to an erect position and, since the rules do not permit lay back, the positive action is for the hips to be forced forwards in towards the barbell. The action is combined with a determined effort to force the shoulders upwards and it is in the latter part of this effort that the muscles of the upper back play a decisive role in achieving the final erect stance. It could be said that the movement of the shoulders backwards is a reaction to the hip drive forwards. However, since the movement will be slow, the action/reaction advantages will be very minimal. The key word, again, to describe one's approach to this lift is determination.

In the final finishing position (*photograph 6*) the knees are locked, the head is held up, the chest is high and the shoulders are braced.

Some of the more experienced lifters adopt a starting position which shows a considerable variation to the one previously described. In this technique the feet are placed very wide apart and the bar is gripped with a comparatively narrow hand spacing, with the arms between the knees. The mechanical implications of the lift are altered. Due to the wide foot stance the shins are vertical at the beginning of the lift, the hips are closer to the bar and the shoulders are directly over the bar. This gives the lifter the opportunity to exert a vertical pull directly from the floor.

At the same time, however, this throws a greater emphasis on the muscles of the front of the thighs and because of the more upright position there will not be the same opportunity for load sharing with the back. It would appear, therefore, that this is a technique which can be employed with advantage by those lifters who display especially high levels of leg power.

6. Finishing position for the two-hands dead lift

Basic principles

Because of the very nature of the lifts, the powerlifter does not have to spend so much of his time on technique training. This does not mean that there is no technique in powerlifting, but techniques can be learned early on in one's career and they do not have to be drastically changed.

Since the power man is not permitted to move his feet during the execution of the lifts, it can be argued that his starting position is of vital important because he will not be allowed to readjust once he begins.

Good body positions are essential. Their teaching is based on sound mechanical and anatomical principles and the need to discipline oneself to maintain these positions must be instilled in all lifters.

Factors affecting the powerlifter

Fitness

What is fitness? A suitable definition is 'the ability to perform a particular piece of work' with success. Having made this very simple statement, it can obviously be elaborated.

It is probably the key to all physical activity and anyone who ignores this will soon be doomed to failure. Please read carefully the section on fitness for power-lifters.

Strength

Strength is the foundation of the sport of powerlifting. Nothing can be left to chance and the lifter must work on an all-round strength building programme. Strength must be developed progressively.

Speed

Coupled with agility and added to strength, speed will produce great power. It is an important aspect that must not be ignored.

Power

This must be developed together with strength, and the powerlifter should undertake some form of explosive movements, such as jumping and sprinting.

Coaching

Coaching is vital to the success of a lifter in any competition. Coaching powerlifters is a question of understanding human relationships, combining it with sound proven principles and experience and imparting all this to your lifter. Coaches are also under stress in the big competitions and a wrong decision by them at a crucial moment can mean the difference between winning and losing.

Conclusion

Willpower, motivation, dedication, determination and courage are all important factors that a good coach will take into consideration. He will use his psychological expertise to get the best out of his athlete and through experience will know when to drive him hard, when to ease him up and when to rest him.

We must always strive to develop these valuable qualities together. Remember, winning is in the mind and a single-minded approach is vital.

Training and preparation for powerlifters

It is obvious that for the majority of lifters it is advisable to look at any one year as a whole before one can begin to plan any sensible and progressive method of training. Even then, training will be quite varied, depending on the quality and experience of the competitor and his eventual goal. Therefore, the novice may well have as his aim the county championship or some other minor competition, whereas an advanced lifter might be aiming for a national title or a world championship place.

Novice competitors

The objective is the progressive development of power, although there is also some small skill element attached to the three power lifts. Novices do not, therefore, have to devise and practise specific skill exercises.

Warming up

Warming up is probably the most neglected part of any form of training with weights. If it is important for experienced lifters, it is absolutely vital for beginners who may well be weak, stiff, unfit, unco-ordinated and inactive.

The warm up should cover all the musculature and joints. Listed below are a few exercises that may be incorporated in the warm up:

arms circling backwards; alternate arms swinging upwards; arms raising sideways and upwards; trunk circling; trunk bending forwards; side bending; alternate toe

MONDAY AND WEDNESDAY EXERCISE	Sets	Reps
High pulls	3	8
Upright rowing	3	8
Back squats	6	8
Press on bench	6	8
Press behind neck	3	8
Triceps stretch	3	8
Abdominal work (sit-ups)	3	10–15
FRIDAY		
Power cleans	3	8
Front squats	6	8
Dead lift	6	8
Shrugs	3	8
Seated incline D/B press	3	8
Hyper-extensions	3	8
Abdominal work (D/B side bends)	3	10

Basic schedule

touching with feet astride; good morning exercise; prone lying – head and shoulders raising; prone lying – legs raising; astride jumping; skip jumping to crouch; lunges; squats; sit-ups; v-sits; short sprints.

Later, the warm up can form part of the fitness training programme.

Training schedule
Monday, Wednesday and Friday have always been popular training days for weightlifters and this seems ideal for the novice powerlifter. It allows the athlete to work hard and then to follow this with a day's rest and recovery.

Lifters should make sure that good body positions are maintained and that technique is never sacrificed for extra weight at this stage.

The lifter should not be too anxious to increase poundages in the early stages and should make sure that each repetition is performed in good style.

Between 15 and 18 days before his first competition, give the lifter a maximum try out and use his best poundages as a guide for his second competition attempt. For example, if his best squat in the try out is 100kg, you should aim at this for his second attempt in the competition.

All other powerlifters
The lifter is now ready to move on to a more advanced stage of training. There will be a reduction in the number of repetitions performed in each set and an increase in poundages and sets. He will start to specialise and concentrate on specific exercises for individual weaknesses.

Planning will become more important and the coach will no longer be able to train athletes on a block principle. It is at this stage that he will need to know his lifters thoroughly and understand all their mental and physical needs.

An extra training session can be introduced and it would seem that Sunday morning would be an appropriate time. This could be a fitness training or games training period or, nearer competition time, an additional power training session.

Apart from novice powerlifters, it is not necessary to divide lifters into intermediate and advanced ability groups for training purposes. Once the basics have been learned, training for all powerlifters can go along very similar lines. The only difference will be in the athletes' sporting calendar, e.g. some lifters will be making divisional championships their objective, whilst others may be aiming at national or even world championships.

The training cycle for the powerlifter for each major competition need only be broadly divided into two phases.

MONDAY	Sets	Reps
Upright rowing	3	8
Press behind neck	3	8
Narrow stance squats	5	6–8
Seated incline D/B press	5	6–8
Shrugs	3	8
Screw curls	3	8
Abdominals (bent leg sit-ups)	5	20
WEDNESDAY		
Power cleans	3	8
Bent over rowing	3	8
Narrow grip bench press	5	8
Front squats	5	8
Round back good morning	3	8
Triceps exercise	3	8
D/B side bends	3	10
FRIDAY		
High pulls	3	8
Bent arm pullover	3	8
Leg press	3	8
Leg curls	3	8
Straight leg dead lift	4	6–8
Bench press	3	8
Hyper-extensions	5	8–10

Exercises should be performed quickly, and rest periods between sets should be cut to a minimum. The objective is to increase muscular endurance so that lifters may be able to withstand the very heavy work loads that are to follow. This is the coach's responsibility and he should observe any specific weaknesses and work on them.

Preparation phase schedule

1 The preparation phase
The length of this phase will depend on the number of major competitions for which the lifter is preparing. The national squad lifter, for example, will probably compete three times a year: at his divisional championships, at the nationals and, hopefully, at the world championship, whereas a lifter of lesser quality may only compete twice: at county and divisional levels.

Body building exercises should play a major part at this stage of training and some fitness and endurance should also be worked on. There should be no emphasis on the competition lifts, but assistance exercises, such as narrow stance squats, narrow grip bench presses and straight-legged dead lifts, would be incorporated. This period would take the lifter to within 8 weeks of the competition and his body weight would be at approximately competition weight.

2 Competition phase
Olympic lifters also add a third stage, called the transitional period, to their training cycle. If powerlifters were to have another phase it could be called the rest phase, but it is not necessary to label it as long as it is understood. At the completion of a competition most powerlifters will go into a resting phase anyway. The pressure is off and there is nothing to worry about in the immediate future; in practice, training will be either light or non-existent. Some even take a complete holiday and return refreshed for a new preparation phase. This varies considerably from lifter to lifter and coaches would do well to observe lifters' preferences.

Training plan for powerlifters
Preparation phase
This phase will depend on the exact date of any competition, but is unlikely ever to exceed 12 weeks and in most cases will be 8–10 weeks.

The emphasis should be on body building exercises and training on weights 3 times a week.

Competition phase

MONDAY OR DAY 1	Sets	Reps
Squats (competition stance)	2	5
knee wraps	2	3
knee wraps	2	2
Bench press (competition position)	3	3
	2	2
	3	1
Dead lift	1	5
	1	3
Straps	3	1
Abdominal work and stretching exercises		

WEDNESDAY OR DAY 2		
Power cleans	3	3
Triceps exercise	3	5
Round back good morning	3	5
Seated incline D/B press	3	5
Press behind neck	1	5
	2	3
Abdominal work		

FRIDAY OR DAY 3		
Squats (competition stance)	1	5
	1	3
	2	2
	3	1
Bench press (competition position)	1	5
	2	3
	2	2
Dead lift	1	6
	1	4
	2	3
Abdominal work		

SUNDAY OR DAY 4

If the fourth training session is included each week, it should take the form of day 2 or, alternatively, it can be used for specific exercises, such as grip work and short range power movements, i.e. half squats, dead lift from boxes and dead lift standing on blocks.

Competition phase schedule

BASIC ANATOMY

Before commencing with a detailed study of the bones, joints and muscles of the human body, it will be useful to have a closer look at the term 'human anatomy'.

If the term is considered in its broadest sense, it will be found to cover the various structures of the body and the factors that influence the structures. However, it will soon be realised that such a broad conception would cover far too wide a field to meet the needs of the potential instructor or coach. Advantage here, therefore, will be taken of systematic anatomy, which as the name implies arranges the various structures in a number of systems or groups in accordance with the functions they perform.

To meet the immediate needs of the instructor it is intended to deal in detail with three such systems:

(a) osteology or the bony system;
(b) arthrology or the joints;
(c) myology or the muscular system.

The bony system

By way of introduction to the detailed study of the bony system let's consider a few general points in outline.

What is the skeleton? It is a framework comprising a series of bones supplemented in parts by cartilage. Many of these bones have both definite and combined functions to perform. For example, there are those which support the weight of the body; those which give protection to underlying structures; those which perform the function of levers; and those which provide a surface for the attachment of muscles.

Classification of bones

Fundamentally, bones may be divided into four classes:

(a) long
(b) short
(c) flat
(d) irregular.

(a) Long bones are found in the upper and lower limbs, and they function as levers. Each possesses a shaft and two ends. Usually the ends are expanded for the purpose of articulation (joint forming) and muscular attachment.

(b) Short bones can be located on the hands and feet, for example where strength, compactness and reasonably restricted movement are needed.

(c) Flat bones are usually found where the basic requirement is to protect underlying structures or to provide a broad surface for muscular attachment. In the latter case the scapula or shoulder blade is an excellent example.

(d) Irregular bones, as the term implies, covers those bones which present varied features, for example, the innominate bones of the pelvic girdle.

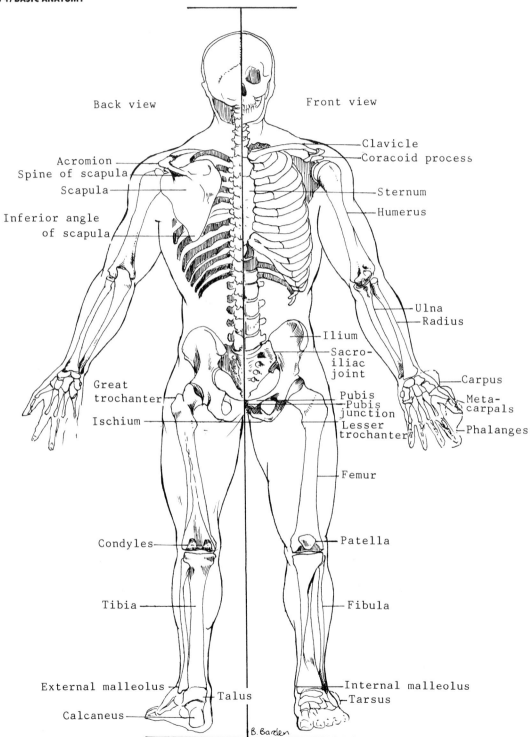

Back view   Front view

Clavicle
Coracoid process

Acromion
Spine of scapula
Scapula

Sternum
Humerus

Inferior angle
of scapula

Ulna
Radius

Ilium
Sacro-
iliac
joint

Great
trochanter

Carpus

Meta-
carpals

Pubis
Pubis
junction
Lesser
trochanter

Ischium

Phalanges

Femur

Condyles

Patella

Tibia

Fibula

External malleolus

Talus

Internal malleolus
Tarsus

Calcaneus

B. Barden

Skeleton: anterior and posterior views

Bones of the lower extremity

The bones of the lower extremity are connected to the trunk by means of the pelvic girdle. The bones comprising this group are:

Feet (phalanges, metatarsals, tarsals)
Tibia
Fibula
Patella
Femur
Pelvic girdle

The feet

The phalanges (fourteen in number) or toes are shorter than those of the hand. The metatarsal bones (five in number) lie behind the phalanges and in front of the tarsals. The tarsals (seven in number) lie behind the metatarsals, and there are two of particular interest, the talus and the calcaneum. The talus can be described as the principle connecting link between the feet and bones of the lower leg; it also plays an important part in the formation of the ankle joint. The calcaneum or heel bone, which is the largest and strongest bone of the tarsal group, has the insertion of the common tendon of the calf muscles.

The tibia

The tibia or shin bone is the innermost bone of the lower leg and is the stronger of the two leg bones. It possesses a shaft and two ends; excluding the femur, it is the longest bone of the skeleton.

The upper end of tibia articulates (forms a joint) with the lower end of the femur. As a general feature, it is expanded in shape to afford a good surface for the body weight to be transmitted through the lower end of the femur. The shaft is triangular in section, and in the lower part is found a sharp crest, better known as the shin. The lower end is also expanded and articulates both with the

fibula and talus in the formation of the ankle joint.

The fibula

The fibula is the outermost bone of the lower leg, and is quite slender compared with the tibia. The upper end is slightly expanded and articulates with the outer condyle (a rounded process) of the tibia; it is important to note that it does not articulate with the femur. The shaft, being very slender, functions mainly for the attachment of muscles. The lower end projects further down than the level of the tibia and, with the tibia, it articulates with the talus in the formation of the ankle joint.

The patella

The patella is perhaps better known as the knee cap. It is flat and triangular in shape and is found within the tendon of the quadriceps muscle group. It enters into the formation of the knee joint by means of an articulating surface on the femur.

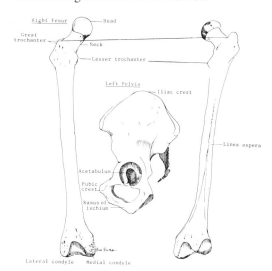

Features of bone: femur and pelvis

The femur

The femur or thigh bone is the longest and strongest bone in the body. The upper end or head is semi-spherical and fits into the cup-shaped hollow on the hip-bone, known as the acetabulum, thus forming the hip joint. Other general features are the greater and lesser trochanters which are roughly shaped processes. The shaft is rounded in shape; on the posterior surface is a well-marked ridge called the linea aspera to which a number of muscles are attached. The lower end is expanded to provide a good bearing surface for transmission of the body weight through the upper surface of the tibia; this end also enters into the formation of the knee joint.

The pelvic girdle

The pelvic girdle is formed by the two innominate bones and wedged between them are the sacrum and the coccyx. The innominate bones are irregular in shape and are composed of three conjoined bones, the ilium or hip bone, the pubis in front and the ischium (this is the most posterior bone).

Briefly, the ilium at the upper end is rather expanded, and forms the iliac crest, and there is also an articulating surface for the sacrum. The pubis, which forms the front part of the hip bone is somewhat triangular in outline; the ischium, which forms the lower part of the hip bone, is well known to us as it is this bone that we sit upon.

As already described, the common factor between all three bones is that they enter into the formation of the cup-shaped cavity called the acetabulum. This receives the head of the femur, thus forming the hip joint.

The sacrum and coccyx will be described in the section dealing with the spine.

Bones of the upper extremity

The bones of the upper extremity are attached to the trunk by means of the shoulder girdle, which consists of the clavicle and the scapula. The bones in this group are:

Hand:
  phalanges
  metacarpals
  carpals
Ulna
Radius
Humerus
Clavicle
Scapula

The hand

The phalanges (fourteen in number) refer to the fingers; the metacarpals (five in number) enter in the formation of the palm; and the carpals (eight in number) are the bones of the wrist.

The ulna

The ulna is the innermost bone of the forearm. The upper end has two processes of particular interest, the olecranon process and the coronoid process. The olecranon process is found on the uppermost part of the upper end and is beak-form in shape. It fits into the olecranon fossa (a depression in a bone) of the lower end of the humerus when the elbow is extended. The coronoid process fits into the coronoid fossa of the humerus when the elbow is flexed; this process is shaped in a bracket-like projection. Finally, the lower end articulates with the humerus and radius in the formation of the elbow joint. The shaft is triangular in shape, giving attachment to the muscles which pronate and supinate the forearm, and also to those which control the movement of the wrist and fingers. The lower end is slightly expanded and comprises a rounded head which articulates with the inner side of the lower end of the radius entering into the radio-ulna joint; the styloid process is a short, rounded projection which is found on the lower end of the ulna.

The radius

The radius is the outermost bone of the

forearm; it is shorter at the head than the ulna. The upper end is expanded, but is narrower than the lower end, presenting a disc-shaped head which articulates with the humerus on its upper surface and with the ulna at the sides. A general feature to note is the biceps tubercle (a smaller process) to which the tendon of the biceps muscle is inserted. The shaft is triangular in section, rather narrow above but widening rapidly towards the lower end. The lower end, as stated above, is the widest part of the radius, entering into the formation of two joints: firstly, two of the carpal bones enter into the formation of the wrist joint and, secondly, the head of the ulna enters in the formation of the inferior radio-ulna joint.

The humerus
The humerus is the longest and largest bone of the upper limb. The upper end comprises a semi-spherical head and two tuberosities (broad, rough processes). The head articulates with the glenoid cavity of the scapula in the formation of the shoulder joint. Below the head is a slightly constricted part known as the anatomical neck. The greater tuberosity is found to the outer side, and below the neck, and the lesser tuberosity is found to the front. The well-known bicipital groove separates the two tuberosities. The shaft is rounded in its upper part, but becomes triangular on section to almost the lower end of the bone. On the back of the shaft is a groove for the radial nerve, and on the outer side, a little above the middle, is the deltoid tuberosity receiving the insertion of the deltoid muscle. The lower end is broad and flat, articulating with the radius and ulna in the formation of the elbow joint. General features include the coronoid fossa, which receives the coronoid process of the ulna when the elbow is bent, and the olecranon fossa, which receives the olecranon process of the ulna when the elbow is extended.

The clavicle
The clavicle or collar bone is a long, gently curved bone that forms the anterior part of the shoulder girdle. Generally speaking, it acts as a prop to brace the shoulder back, and to transmit some of the weight of the limb to the trunk. There are two ends, the inner or sternal end, which articulates with the sternum in the formation of the sterno-clavicular joint, and the outer, or acromial extremity, which articulates with the acromion process of the scapula in the formation of the acromio-clavicular joint.

The scapula
The scapula forms the posterior part of the shoulder girdle; it is a large and flattened triangular bone covering parts of the second to the seventh ribs. The scapula presents several interesting features:

(1) the two surfaces: the anterior or coastal surface is found to lie nearest the ribs, and the posterior, or dorsal surface, which can be easily distinguished by its prominent ridge of bone, is termed the spine of the scapula;

(2) the three angles: the superior angle lies at the junction of the superior and vertebral borders; the inferior angle is the lowest point of the scapula and lies over the seventh rib (when the arm is raised it can be seen to pass forwards round the chest wall); and the lateral angle is thick and broad and can be located in the section bearing the glenoid cavity;

(3) the three borders: the superior border is thin and sharp and is the shortest of the borders (it extends from the superior angle to the base of the corocoid process); the vertebral border extends from the inferior to the superior angle; the axillary border extends from the inferior angle to the glenoid cavity.

The thorax

The thorax is formed by the twelve thoracic vertebrae at the back, the twelve pairs of ribs at the sides and the sternum at the front.

The sternum or breast bone is a long, flat bone comprising three parts. The manubrium sterni is triangular in shape and is placed above the main body. It articulates at the upper and outer sides with the sternal ends of the clavicles. At the sides proper the first pair of ribs articulate with the manubrium, and the second pair articulate at the junction of the manubrium and the body of the sternum. The body of the sternum is narrower and longer than the manubrium with which it articulates at the sternal angle. At the lower end it narrows and articulates with the xiphoid process. The sides are notched for the attachment of the third, fourth, fifth, sixth and seventh ribs. The xiphoid process is the smallest part and sometimes it varies in shape.

The thoracic vertebrae are dealt with in detail under the section on the spine, but in this context it should be noted that they form part of the thorax by affording facets and transverse processes on the vertebrae to which the twelve pairs of ribs are attached.

The ribs

Each rib has two ends and a shaft. There are twelve pairs of ribs and they are classified according to their anterior attachments, i.e. true, false and floating.

The upper seven pairs of ribs are termed the true ribs. These are attached behind to the thoracic vertebrae and to the sternum anteriorly by means of their costal cartilages. The lower five pairs are termed false ribs, and are attached to the sternum indirectly by means of the costal cartilages to the cartilage of the rib immediately above. The two lowermost ribs are termed the floating ribs, so-called because they are free at their anterior ends.

The spine

The spine comprises thirty-three vertebrae: seven cervical, twelve thoracic, five lumbar, five sacral and four coccygeal.

The cervical vertebrae: there are seven vertebrae in this group and of these seven the first and second have special functions. The first is termed the atlas and supports the head: the second is called the axis and provides a pivot upon which the atlas and, with it, the head rotate. The remaining five conform with the general pattern of typical vertebrae. A point to note is that the seventh is the first vertebra to possess an undivided spinous process and is noted for its long spine.

The thoracic vertebrae: there are twelve vertebrae in this group and they show a gradual increase in size from the first to the twelfth. Each vertebra articulates with the ribs which encircle the trunk from the thoracic vertebrae to the sternum in front. Compared with the cervical vertebrae, the thoracic vertebrae are larger.

The lumbar vertebrae: there are five lumbar vertebrae in this group, and they can be distinguished from the other vertebrae by their greater size. It can be noted that the fifth lumbar vertebra articulates with the sacrum, forming the lumbo-sacral joint.

The sacrum

There are five vertebrae in this group which are fused together to form a large triangular bone, the sacrum. It is this bone, together with the coccyx, which is wedged between the two innominate bones of the pelvic girdle. The base of the sacrum lies above and articulates with the fifth lumbar vertebra. The sides articulate with the innominate bones and the apex articulates with the coccyx.

The coccyx

There are four vertebrae in this group which are fused together to form a small triangular bone articulating above with the sacrum.

Joints of the skeleton

A sound knowledge of the mechanics of joint function is essential to the understanding of muscular action.

Joints are formed by the meeting of two or more bones which allow free, slight or no movement at all. Joints may, therefore, be classified as follows:

(a) immovable joints;
(b) slightly movable joints;
(c) freely movable joints.

Immovable joints
This type of joint is found where the bones are joined by cartilages or by a system of dovetailed edges.

Slightly movable joints
Joints of this nature consist of two bony surfaces united by ligaments alone or ligaments with a fibrous cartilage interposed between the bony surfaces.

Freely movable joints
In this third class the ends of the bone are covered with cartilage and are connected by a fibrous capsule. The capsule is the synovial membrane which secretes a fluid to lubricate the joint.

Freely movable joints may be classified into six different types:

(i)   gliding – whose flat surfaces are capable of only limited movement;
(ii) hinge – where the articular surfaces are moulded together to permit movement in one plane only;
(iii) pivot – where the movement is limited to rotation;
(iv) condyloid – where the articular surface, or condyle, fits into a concave, articular surface, thus allowing flexion, extension, etc;
(v)   saddle – the movement here is similar to that of the condyloid, but the surfaces are concavo-convex;
(vi) ball and socket – where a spherical head fits into a cup-like cavity and movement is permitted in any direction.

Detailed structure of certain joints

The elbow joint
This joint is formed by the articulation of the lower end of the humerus, the upper extremity of the ulna and the head of the radius. The elbow joint is of the hinge type which permits flexion, or bending of the elbow, and extension, or straightening.

The hip joint
The hip joint is of the ball and socket type and is formed by the cup-shaped cavity of the acetabulum and the head of the femur. Strong ligaments and a capsule surround the joint. The movements permitted are raising of the thigh (flexion); bracing the thigh backwards (extension); raising the thigh sideways, away from the other leg (abduction); moving the thigh from a position of abduction, across the other leg (adduction); rotating the thigh outwards (external rotation); rotating the thigh inwards (internal rotation); circular movement and circumduction.

The knee joint
The knee joint is of the hinge type and is formed by the condyles of the femur and the upper end of the tibia. Considering the length of the leg bones, the knee joint may be thought to be rather weak, but this is not so, due to the powerful ligaments and muscles around the joint.

The movements at the knee joint are flexion or bending of the knee and extension or straightening of the knee.

The shoulder girdle

The two joints of the shoulder girdle are freely movable gliding joints. The joint between the sternum and the clavicle is the only point at which the shoulder girdle articulates with the trunk, and movement of the clavicle is permitted in all directions. The other joint is where the outer end of the clavicle forms and acromio-clavicular joint with the acromion process of the scapula.

Both these joints are supported by strong ligaments, and movements at the shoulder are: forward rotation; bracing back the shoulders or backward rotation; shrugging the shoulders or elevation; and downward movements of the shoulders or depression.

The ankle joint

The ankle joint is a hinge type joint that is formed by the tibia and the fibula which together form a socket to receive the body of the talus. Movements of this joint are dorsi-flexion or bending the foot towards the leg and plantar-flexion or pointing the foot downwards.

Muscles of the skeleton

The attention of readers is drawn especially to the fact that this section is to be considered an introduction to this very interesting aspect of human anatomy.

The system employed lists the muscles in chart form. The name, surface position where applicable, attachments and action of the muscles are given.

Attachments

It has been the custom in the past to name the attachments of a muscle as 'origin' and 'insertion'. This can cause confusion in understanding the true action of a muscle, because it leads one to assume that a muscle can pull only in one direction. A muscle, however, tends to pull equally from its attachments towards its centre.

In this book the following system of naming the attachments has been adopted:

upper attachments	applicable to muscles of the neck and trunk which run more or
lower attachments	less vertically
medial attachments	applicable to muscles which run more or
lateral attachments	less horizontally
proximal attachments	applicable to muscles of or appertaining to
distal attachments	the extremities.

Fundamental movements

The following movements are referred to in the details of the action of a muscle or muscle groups.

flexion	to reduce the angle at the joint
extension	to return from flexion
adduction	to bring towards the midline of the body
abduction	to take away from the midline of the body
elevation	to raise, such as lifting the shoulders
depression	to pull down, such as pulling the shoulders down
lateral flexion	to bend laterally the neck or trunk
rotation	rotary movement about the long axis of the bone: this can be inward and outward, and includes supination and pronation of the forearm when flexed at right angles to the upper arm
circumduction	an orderly circling of a part of the body so that the segment as a whole describes a cone.

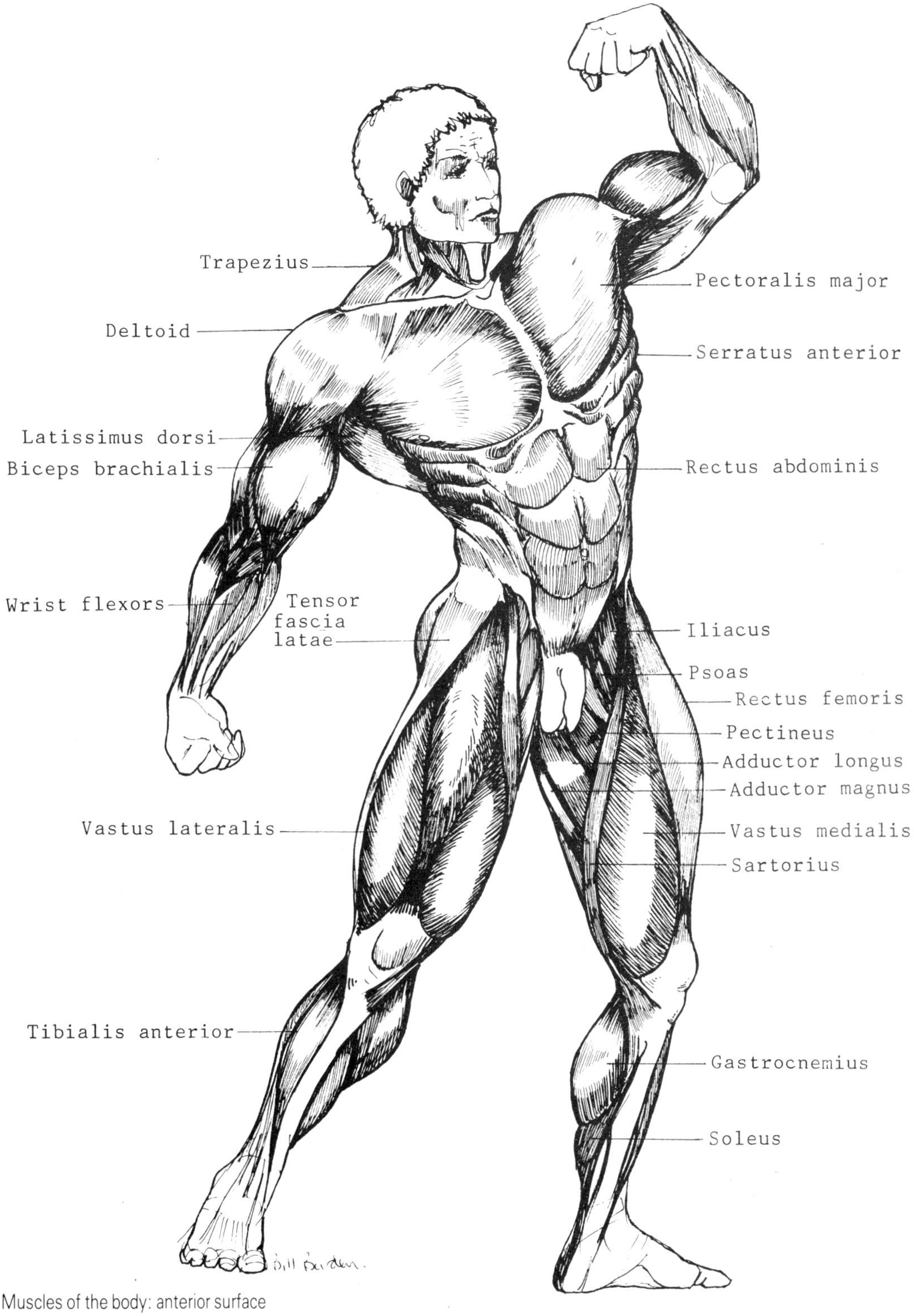

Trapezius

Deltoid

Latissimus dorsi

Biceps brachialis

Wrist flexors

Tensor
fascia
latae

Vastus lateralis

Tibialis anterior

Pectoralis major

Serratus anterior

Rectus abdominis

Iliacus

Psoas

Rectus femoris

Pectineus

Adductor longus

Adductor magnus

Vastus medialis

Sartorius

Gastrocnemius

Soleus

Bill Garden.

Muscles of the body: anterior surface

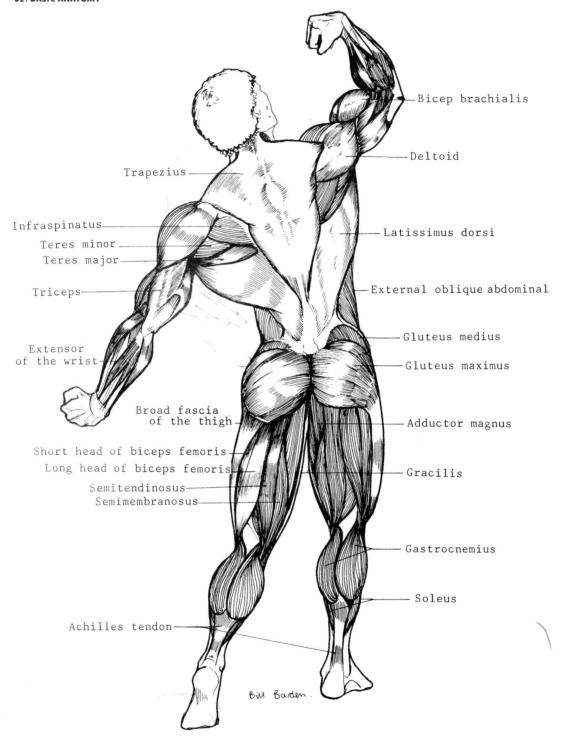

Bicep brachialis

Deltoid

Trapezius

Infraspinatus

Teres minor

Teres major

Triceps

Latissimus dorsi

External oblique abdominal

Extensor
of the wrist

Gluteus medius

Gluteus maximus

Broad fascia
of the thigh

Adductor magnus

Short head of biceps femoris

Long head of biceps femoris

Semitendinosus

Semimembranosus

Gracilis

Gastrocnemius

Soleus

Achilles tendon

Bill Barden.

Muscles of the body: posterior surface

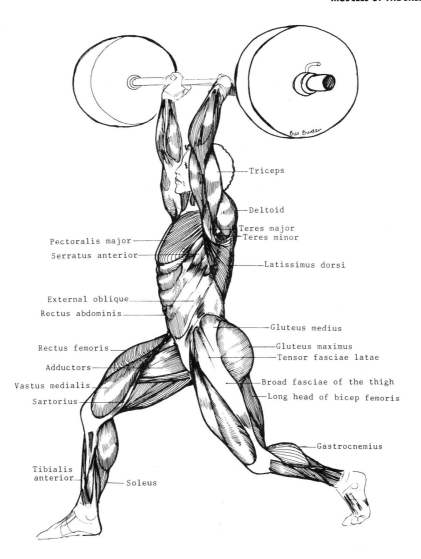

Muscles of the body: lateral and medial surfaces

The following terms referring to the anatomic position are also used:

anterior — to the front
posterior — to the rear
lateral — to the outside away from the midline
medial — to the inside towards the midline

superior — the top aspect
inferior — the bottom aspect

A part may be described in a combination of these terms, e.g. anterior/superior or medial/inferior.

SURFACE POSITION	PROXIMAL ATTACHMENTS	DISTAL ATTACHMENTS	ACTION
SOLEUS			
Back of lower leg. Beneath the gastrocnemius.	Upper surfaces of the posterior aspect of the tibia and fibula(+interosseus membrane)	By calcaneal tendon into calcaneus (Achilles tendon)	Prime mover for plantar flexion of the ankle joint (pointing toes). Running Jumping Calf Raises
GASTROCNEMIUS			
Back of lower leg. Nearest to the surface.	By two tendons from the posterior aspect of the condyles of the femur.	As above.	Prime mover for plantar flexion of the ankle joint in load bearing positions. It is a true flexor of the knee joint. Running jumping calf raises.
TIBIALIS ANTERIOR			
Lateral and anterior aspect of lower leg.	Upper 2/3 of lateral surface of the tibia corresponding portion of the interosseus membrane.	Medial and undersurface of 1st cuneform and base of 1st metatarsal (big toe).	Prime mover for dorsiflexion (lifting foot towards shin) and inversion of the foot at the ankle.

SURFACE POSITION	PROXIMAL ATTACHMENT	DISTAL ATTACHMENT	ACTION
RECTUS FEMORIS			
Anterior aspect of upper leg.	Anterior-inferior spine of ilium and by a second head from a groove above the acetabulum.	Proximal Border of the patella and thereby indirectly via patella ligament to the tuberosity of the tibia.	Prime mover for hip joint flexion. Prime mover for knee joint extension. (Has been called the kicking muscle.) Running, jumping, walking, swimming and lifting.
VASTI MUSCLES			
Lateralis			
Lateral aspect of upper leg.	Lateral surface of the femur just below the greater trochanter and upper half of the linea aspera.		Prime movers for knee extension; the pull of each upon the patella balances the others.
Medialis			
Below the rectus femoris and medial aspect of the upper leg.	Whole length of linea aspera and medial supracondylarline lower half intertrochanteric line.	Proximal border of patella and thereby indirectly via patella ligament into tuberosity of the tibia.	The rectus femoris and vasti muscles are collectively known as the quadriceps femoris.
Intermedius			
Below the rectus femoris.	Anterior and lateral surfaces of upper two thirds of shaft of femur.		Running, jumping, walking, swimming and lifting.
ILIACUS			
Deep muscle.	Anterior surface of ilium and base of sacrum.	Joins with psoas tendon to lesser trochanter of femur.	Flexion of hip joint. Raises trunk to sitting position when feet fixed – raises legs when trunk fixed.
PSOAS			
Deep muscle.	Sides of bodies and intervertebral cartilages of last thoracic and all lumbar vertebrae.	Lesser trochanter of femur with iliacus.	Flexion of hip joint. Raises trunk to sitting position when feet are fixed. Raises legs when trunk is fixed.

Top table on page 84
Muscles involved in plantarflexion and dorsiflexion of the ankle and flexion of the knee

Bottom table on page 84
Muscles involved in flexion of the hip and extension of the knee

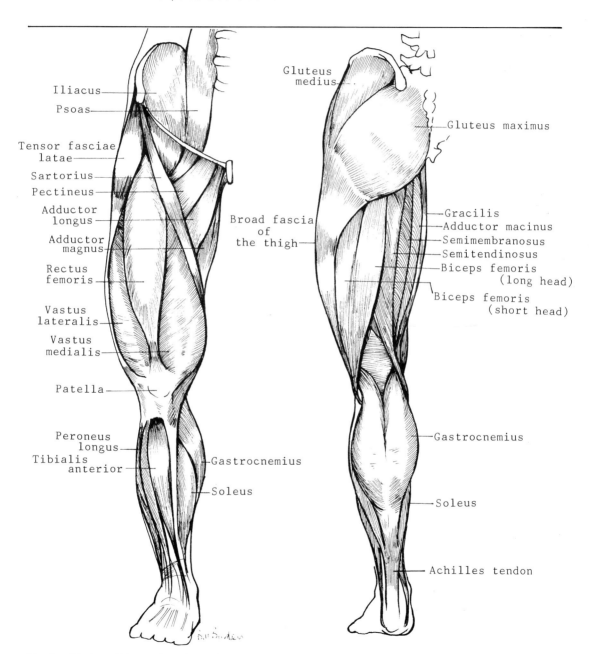

Muscles of the leg and hip: anterior and posterior

SURFACE POSITION	PROXIMAL ATTACHMENT	DISTAL ATTACHMENT	ACTION
BICEPS FEMORIS			
Back of upper leg.	LONG HEAD from tuberosity of ischium. SHORT HEAD lateral lip of linea aspera.	Lateral condyle of tibia and head of fibula.	Long head acts on hip joint, being prime mover for hip extension. Both heads are prime movers for flexion and outward rotation of the knee. Lifting movements from floor – sprinting.
SEMITENDINOSUS			
Back of inner upper leg.	Tuberosity of ischium.	Upper part of medial surface of tibia.	Extends thigh at hip joint. Flexion of the knee joint. Inward rotation of the tibia when knee is flexed. Lifting movement from floor – sprinting.
SEMIMEMBRANOSUS			
Back of inner upper leg.	Tuberosity of ischium.	Posterior surface of medial condyle of tibia.	As for semitendinosus. Lifting movement from floor – sprinting.
GLUTEUS MAXIMUS			
Buttocks.	Outer surface of the ilium on posterior ¼ of its crest. Sacrum close to the ilium, a side of coccyx.	A line 4″ on the posterior aspect of the femur between the greater trochanter and linea-aspera.	Prime mover in raising the trunk from the stooping position. Very important in hip extension. Well developed in lifters, sprinters. Jumping and running.

SURFACE POSITION	PROXIMAL ATTACHMENT	DISTAL ATTACHMENT	ACTION
ADDUCTORS			
Longus			
Medical aspect of the groin.	Anterior surface of the pubis.	Middle half of linea aspera.	
Brevis			
Deep muscle.	Outer surface of ramus of pubis.	From lesser trochanter to linea aspera and upper ¼ of linea aspera.	HIP JOINT ADDUCTION
MAGNUS			
Medial surface of middle half of thigh.	Front of pubis. Tuberosity of ischium. Whole of ramus connecting the above features.	Whole of linea aspera. Medical supracondylar line. Adductor tubercle on medial condyle of femur.	Swimming, horse riding, gymnastics.
GLUTEUS MEDIUS GLUTEUS MINIMUS			
Deep muscles.	Posterior surface of ilium.	Greater trochanter of femur. Anterior and lateral aspects.	HIP JOINT ABDUCTION Inward rotation of femur. Gymnastics and Swimming.

| SURFACE POSITION | ATTACHMENTS | | ACTION |
	LOWER	UPPER	
ERECTOR SPINAE			
Either side of the spine. Many, however, are deep muscles.	These muscles have upper and lower attachments on the lumbar, thoracic and lower cervical vertebrae. The ribs and mastoid process of the temporal bone.		Extension and hyperextension of the head and spine. Side bending of the spine and rotation of the head. Back arching, very strongly employed in all lifting.
QUADRATUS LUMBORUM			
Deep muscle	Crest of ilium.	12 ribs and tips of the transverse process of upper 4 lumbar vertebrae.	Acting single, it flexes the lumbar spine laterally. Back arching and side bending.
RECTUS ABDOMINIS			
Front of abdomen from pubis to sternum.	Crest of pubis.	Cartilages of fifth, sixth and seventh ribs.	BOTH Flexion of thoracic and lumbar spine. ONE Lateral flexion of thoracic and lumbar spine.
INTERNAL OBLIQUE			
Lies on side of abdomen beneath the external oblique.	Lumbar fascia crest of ilium, inguinal ligament.	The cartilages of the 8th, 9th and 10th Ribs. The linea alba, the crest of pubis.	BOTH Flexion of thoracic and lumbar spine. ONE Lateral flexion of thoracic and lumbar spine.
EXTERNAL OBLIQUE			
Lies on side of abdomen.	Anterior ½ of crest of ilium. Crest of pubis and linea alba.	By saw-tooth attachments to lower 8 ribs.	BOTH Flexion of thoracic and lumbar spine. ONE Lateral flexion of thoracic and lumbar spine. All abdominals used in trunk flexion and twisting; all throwing movements.

Muscles of the spine and trunk

Table (top left)
Muscles involved in flexion of the knee and extension of the hip

Table (below left)
Muscles involved in adduction and abduction on the hip

SURFACE POSITION	PROXIMAL ATTACHMENT	DISTAL ATTACHMENT	ACTION
LATISSIMUS DORSI			
Lateral aspect of the back, sweeping up under the arm.	Spinous processes of lower 6 dorsal and all lumbar vertebrae. Back of sacrum crest of ilium. Lower 3 ribs.	Bottom of bicipital grove of humerus. Sometimes attached to inferior angle of scapula.	Active part in all humerus adduction extension and inward rotation. Rope climbing, gymnastics.
RHOMBOID MAJOR AND MINOR			
Deep muscles.	Spinous processes of 7th cervical and first 5 thoracic vertebrae.	Vertebral border of the scapula from spine to the inferior angle.	Draws lower angle of scapula upwards and inwards. Raises scapula. All shoulder elevation.
LEVATOR SCAPULAE			
Deep muscles.	Transverse processes of the upper 4 cervical vertebrae.	Vertebral border of scapula from spine to superior angle.	Elevates the scapula, with shoulder fixed, bends neck to its own side.
SERRATUS ANTERIOR			
Lateral/anterior surface of chest.	Outer surfaces of the upper 9 ribs, at side of chest.	Anterior surface of vertebral border of scapula from superior to inferior angle.	Upward rotation and abduction of scapula round the chest wall. All overhead lifting, punching.
TRAPEZIUS			
Kite-shaped area in upper back, neck and shoulders.	Base of skull, ligament of the neck. Spinous processes of all vertebrae from 7th cervical to 12th thoracic.	Along a curved line on outer posterior border of clavicle. Top of acromium process. Upper border of spine of scapula.	Draws shoulders together and head back. High pulls, upright rowing, bent forward rowing.

Muscles on the back acting upon the shoulder joint and shoulder girdle

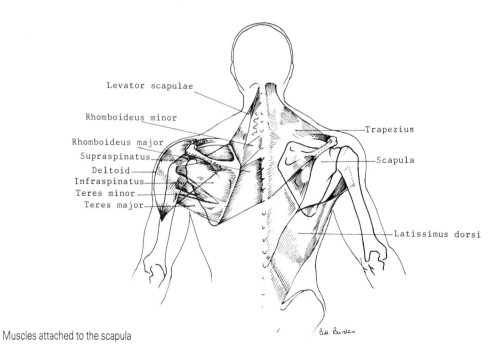

Muscles attached to the scapula

SURFACE POSITION	PROXIMAL ATTACHMENT	DISTAL ATTACHMENT	ACTION
DELTOID			
Anterior Middle Posterior			
This muscle group caps the joint of the upper arm and shoulder.	Along a curved line following the outer ⅓ of the anterior border of the clavicle. Top of the acromion process. Posterior border of spine of scapula.	Deltoid tuberosity on the lateral aspects of the humerus.	A complex muscle group. A powerful abductor of the humerus. Lifting weights overhead. Raising weights: lateral raise, forward raise, bent forward raise. All forms of bench pressing.
SUPRA SPINATUS			
Beneath medial deltoid. Deep muscle.	Inner ⅔ of supra spinatus fossa above spine of scapula.	Top of greater tuberosity of humerus.	Abduction of humerus in conjunction with deltoids.
TERES MAJOR			
Passing under arm pit.	External posterior surface of inferior angle of scapula.	Inner border of bicipital grove of humerus.	Inward rotation of humerus. Works with latissimus dorsi.
TERES MINOR			
Deep muscle.	Dorsal surface of the axillary border of the scapula.	Lower part of greater tuberosity of humerus and adjacent shaft.	Outward rotation of humerus. Works with infraspinatus.
INFRASPINATUS			
Posterior surface of the scapula.	Posterior surface of the scapula beneath the spine of scapula.	Middle of greater tuberosity of humerus.	Outward rotation of humerus. Works with teres minor.
SUBSCAPULARIS			
Beneath scapula adjacent to rib cage.	Whole of anterior surface of scapula.	Lesser tuberosity of humerus.	Inward rotation of humerus. Antagonist to the teres minor and to the infraspinatus.

Muscles acting on the shoulder joint

SURFACE POSITION	PROXIMAL ATTACHMENTS	DISTAL ATTACHMENTS	ACTION
PECTORALIS MAJOR			
Large muscle on the front of upper chest.	Inner ⅔ of anterior border of clavicle, the sternum and the first 6 ribs.	By a flat tendon approx. 3 inches wide to the ridge which forms the outer border of the bicipital grove of the humerus.	Adduction of the upper arm. Inward rotation of the upper arm. Bench pressing. Lateral raise – lying. Pullovers. Javelin and discus, gymnastics. Swimming.
PECTORALIS MINOR			
Lies beneath the pectoralis minor.	Anterior surfaces of ribs 3, 4 and 5.	Tip of coracoid process of scapula.	Elevates ribs, assists serratus anterior to draw scapula forward round chest wall.
STERNO-MASTOID (STERNOCLEIDOMASTOID)			
On the side and front of neck.	By 2 heads, from top of sternum and medial ⅓ of clavicle.	Mastoid process of the skull.	BOTH HEADS Flexion of the neck. ONE HEAD Lateral flexion, rotation to opposite side.

Muscles of the chest acting on the shoulder joint, front of the neck

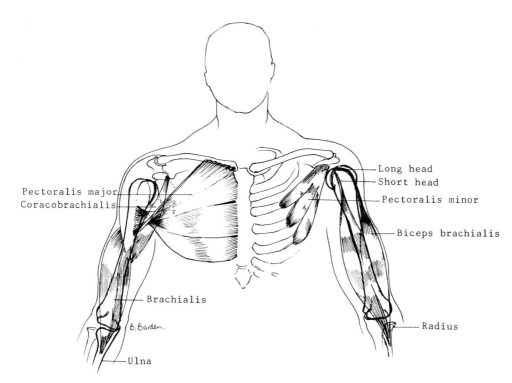

Muscles of the chest and upper arms

SURFACE POSITION	PROXIMAL ATTACHMENT	DISTAL ATTACHMENT	ACTION
BICEPS: 2 HEADS			
Front of upper arm.	Long head: from scapula at top of glenoid fossa. Short head: from coracoid process of scapula.	Bicipital tuberosity of radius in forearm.	Can act on 3 joints: shoulder, elbow and radio/ulna. Powerful supinator of the forearm; elbow flexor. Weak flexor of shoulder joint. Dumbell screw curls.
BRACHIALIS			
Over elbow joint at the front beneath the biceps.	Anterior surface of lower ½ of humerus.	Tuberosity of ulna and anterior surface of coronoid process.	True flexor of the elbow joint.
TRICEPS: 3 HEADS			
Back of the upper arm.	Long head from the infraglenoid tuberosity of the scapula. Lateral head from the posterior surface of upper ½ of the humerus. Medial head from the posterior surface of lower ⅔ of the humerus.	Olecranon process of the ulna.	Extension of forearm at elbow joint. (Long head, extension and hyperextension of humerus at shoulder joint.) All pressing work and exercises in which the elbow is extended against resistance.
COROCOBRACHIALIS			
Deep muscle.	Coracoid process of scapula.	Inner middle surface of humerus.	Draws the arm forwards and inwards.
BRACHIORADIALIS			
Radial aspect of front of upper half of forearm.	Lateral lower end of the humerus.	Lateral side of the base of the styloid process of the radius.	Flexion of the elbow joint.

Muscles which flex and extend the elbow and assist with shoulder joint flexion/extension

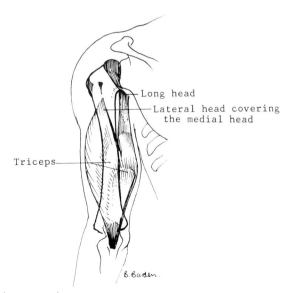

Long head
Lateral head covering the medial head
Triceps
B. Barden.

Triceps (muscle at the rear of the upper arm)

PRINCIPLES OF KINETICS

Kinesiology is the science of human motion; it selects from relevant sciences those principles which assist in the analysis of physical activity. Within the compass of this book, however, the chapter is headed 'principles of kinetics' because it is only possible to deal briefly with the principles.

Muscle work

Under this heading a muscle, or muscle group, is considered in the light of whether it shortens, lengthens or holds a fixed position.

Concentric contraction

In this case the muscle actually shortens against resistance. For example, consider the first part of the two-hands curl. The flexors of the elbow, the brachialis and biceps receive a message from the brain via a motor nerve commanding them to contract. The insertion, being on the forearm bones, is brought towards the origin by the active shortening of those muscles, and they are therefore said to be working concentrically.

Eccentric contraction

The return from shortening to the muscle's normal length is called eccentric contraction. It is said to be active lengthening against resistance, but the term lengthening should be used with caution, because as was said above the muscle really returns to its normal length. However, taking the two hands-curl again, consider the second half

of the lowering movement. When the weight is lowered from the finishing position, down comes another message telling the same muscles (the elbow flexors) to relax gradually. Gravity pulls the weight towards the ground, and the muscles actively lengthen against the resistance of the weight, until it arrives once more at the starting position. Therefore, the muscles are, in this case, working eccentrically to lower the bar.

Static contraction

When a muscle is actively engaged in holding a static position, i.e. without changing its length, it is said to be working statically. Thus, if in the two-hands curl the bar was checked half-way through the movement, then the muscles would be working statically to hold the position.

It is now possible to give a generalisation and to say that in barbell and dumb-bell exercises the muscles actively engaged in raising the weight work concentrically and in the lowering of the weight they work eccentrically. If the weight were checked in any position, then static contraction would result.

Muscle action

Closely allied to muscle work is the function of a muscle which contributes to the actual movement, whether it is checking unnecessary movement or steadying or stabilising a bone. Under this heading the following terms are used: prime movers; antagonists; synergists and fixators.

Prime movers or agonists

A prime mover is a muscle which is principally responsible for the movement taking place. In most movements there are usually several muscles involved, but basically any movement may be said to have a principal mover and those helping to perform the movement are collectively called the assistant mover.

For example, consider the hold out in front raised. In raising the bar from the thighs the anterior deltoid is the principal mover. In the case of the two-hands curls, the agonists would be the brachialis and biceps, and in the bent arm pull over, the triceps.

Antagonists

Basically, an antagonist is a muscle which causes the opposite movement from that of the muscle described under prime movers.

In the two-hands curl it was stated above that the elbow flexors were the prime movers; the muscle which is on the opposite side and has the opposite action is the triceps, so the triceps is the antagonist.

Important note

It is necessary at this stage to point out that a muscle or muscle group can act either as a prime mover or as an antagonist. To gain a clear understanding of this the following should be read most carefully.

In the two-hands curl the elbow flexors are the prime movers and the triceps are the antagonists, whereas in the bent arm pull over the triceps become the prime movers and the elbow flexors become the antagonists.

Synergists

Whilst the term covers several functions, in this context it is intended to imply the basic principle of checking unnecessary movement.

A muscle may cross one or more joints; when it does so, it is capable of movement at every joint it crosses. This, however, is not always desirable and therefore synergic muscle action provides the necessary check.

A classic example is found in the hand. The flexors of the fingers cross many joints, including the palm side of the wrist. When an object is picked up or a sponge is squeezed, there is a tendency to flex the wrist as well as the fingers. Therefore, the extensors of the wrist, on the knuckle side, act as a brake, allowing the flexors of the fingers to act on the fingers without flexing the wrist. In this example it is the wrist extensors which are acting as synergists.

Fixators

One of the main functions of fixators is the fixing of the origin of the muscles. During the performance of the forward bend rowing motion exercise, the hip extensors (gluteus maximus, hamstrings and erector spinae) act as fixators in fixing the origin of the latissimus dorsi whilst it works as the prime mover in bringing the arms upwards and backwards to touch the body with the bar.

In the biceps exercise with dumb-bells, where the arms are held in the sideways stretch position, the elbows are then bent and straightened while the deltoid holds the upper arms stationary and parallel to the floor. In fixing the origin of the biceps and brachialis the deltoid acts as a fixator.

It will now be appreciated that, depending on the movement, a muscle or muscle group may work concentrically or statically. Also, a muscle may act as a prime mover, an antagonist, a synergist or a fixator.

Range of movement

Normal, healthy muscles have the ability to work from full extension of a joint to full flexion. This means that they have a full range of movement.

For convenience, the range of movement will be described under the following headings:

(a)   inner range,
(b)   middle range,
(c)   outer range.

Inner range

The inner range occurs at the completion of the last third of the movement where the insertion is brought nearest to the attachment of origin, and is, therefore, where the muscle is working at its shortest length.

For examples of this inner range consider the elbow flexors during the near completion of the two-hands curl; the triceps during the completion of the two-hands press or press on back; the quadriceps during the latter few inches of attaining the erect position from the deep knee bend, and so on.

Middle range

The heading is really self-explanatory: this range is found in the position where the muscle is neither at its shortest nor longest length, i.e. it is passing through the midway position of full range.

The middle range of an exercise usually causes some difficulty, because it is in this range that the function of leverage is unfavourable.

Examples are relatively easy to detect in practice, although the reader is advised not to become confused by faulty technique which may mislead the location of the middle range of an exercise.

Outer range

It is in this range that the muscle is working at its greatest length in the first third of the movement.

Examples of the outer range are relatively simple, provided the reader has a fair knowledge of prime movers of the exercise being performed: elbow flexors in the two-hands curl; triceps in the bent arm pull over, and so on.

Before concluding, attention is drawn to certain exercises which do not seem to come under the principle of middle range. Detailed study, however, will disclose that such movements are not full-range.

In the hold out in front raised from below, the most difficult part of the movement is the completion, i.e. a lift. This is because as a movement it falls short of the full range of movement of deltoid work and is, in fact, only about the mid-range of work as the thighs to arms stretch upwards.

Once the reader has grasped the concept that there are relatively easy and hard ranges of exercise, then advanced exercises to develop muscles in all three ranges can be readily mapped out. Consider the press on back: even with a heavy weight it is comparatively easy to get the weight moving and the elbows off the floor. This is because the muscles involved are acting as prime movers in their outer range. Once the middle range is reached, the problem of leverage occurs, but on reaching the inner range little difficulty is usually met in locking the elbows.

TEACHING PRINCIPLES

The instructor

Perhaps the prime requirement of any instructor is to be firmly convinced of the value of the work he is teaching, and this must be proven by whole-hearted enthusiasm.

The more experience the instructor has as a teacher, the more it will be realised that he can only expect to get out of a class what he, the instructor, is prepared to put in.

No instructor should ever degenerate into a lifeless image, mechanically grinding out orders and getting through a schedule in a set manner. He should have a firm belief in the subject being taught, and should radiate a genuine keenness and enthusiasm.

It is surprising how infectious the manner of an instructor can be as a stimulant to pupils. To maintain this effect it is important that the programme of exercises is well prepared beforehand. This should ensure that there is no chance of any 'dead' points creeping into the session whilst the instructor is struggling to remember the next exercise. Once such a situation is allowed to arise, the pupils will soon lose faith in both instruction and instructor.

Interest should be the key note of all teaching. The instructor must keep it concise and informative, and on no account should he ever give a lecture.

Teaching technique

There are many variations in applying methods used in teaching. In weightlifting and weight training, however, three well defined stages of progress lend themselves to a suitable division for detailed discussion. These stages are those of the beginner, intermediate and advanced pupils. The following sections will consider each of these stages, with a technique suitable for application. In the present section, only the general principles will be considered.

The beginner

For the pupil being introduced to the use of weights for the first time, there is a definite need for a concise, yet informative, and coaxing approach. The teaching sequence advocated on page 98 will be found to be especially suitable for beginners. This is because the sequence provides excellent continuity for dealing with each and every stage of the exercise (instructors will also find this sequence very useful for introducing new exercises to pupils with experience). Assessing correct poundages, suited to capabilities and age, should be determined accurately. The principle is quite simple: the pupil is tested on certain fundamental exercises, and his strength and ability are ascertained. Using the assessed poundages, the instructor can place the pupil on a set of exercises designed to exercise the muscle groups and joints over their full range of movement.

Intermediate pupils

Once a pupil has completed his basic training, in order to maintain his interest it is imperative that a different type of pro-gramme, designed to follow up progressively the fundamental training, be introduced. Usually, by the time this stage is reached, pupils have a reasonable knowledge, and ability, to perform most of the basic exercises. The instructor benefits here, because he is able to dispense with certain preliminary descriptions: he can simply name the exercise and repetitions to be performed, and so leave more time to be devoted to actual coaching.

At this point special attention must be given to the grading of pupils. It should be done according to strength and capability and in a way that does not dishearten students with weaker ability, as is often the case in mixed classes.

Grading and grouping are very varied and depend entirely on the ambition and interest of each pupil. This aspect of an instructor's ability must be carefully employed and he must be capable of showing competence in dealing with individual requirements.

The attention of the instructor is particularly drawn to the fact that success in ability group teaching depends on a common sense attitude to orderliness and neatness. Equipment and groups must be arranged so that members of each section may work on their routine without distracting others, which would be the case if the pupils were scattered in the club irrespective of ability and purpose.

Advanced pupils

At the advanced stage the instructor should be dealing with pupils who have completed both their fundamental and intermediate training. The pupils' knowledge, as well as their performance, should have increased progressively. This should leave the instructor with even more time for constructive coaching. A conversational tone of command can now be safely introduced.

It is at this stage that the knowledge of the competent instructor is put to the test. No longer can he generalise in his instruction, since there is a need to observe every detail: major faults must be corrected, and even the smallest ones must be ironed out. The challenge must be accepted with drive and enthusiasm: nothing less is satisfactory, and the instructor would do well to remember that the moulding of a pupil's future in a chosen field could be decided at this crucial stage.

Use of the voice

The use of the voice is very important in teaching, and here it is intended to cover the general principles as applied to the different techniques.

By varying the sound of the voice, instructors can indicate how the movement is to be performed, such as slowly, quickly, strongly or rhythmically. Also, a class in a bad position can be halted by simply altering the tone of the voice.

Commands may be divided into three parts:

(a) cautionary
(b) pause
(c) executive.

The cautionary word of command is used to warn pupils that care is required to perform a certain exercise.

Pausing should be a deliberate way of ensuring that the slower pupils are given the opportunity to grasp what has been said.

The executive part of the command is that upon which the pupils act, i.e. it is at this stage that the instructor indicates, by tone of voice, how he wishes the movement to be performed.

It is surprising how many students (even those with many years of experience), when attending residential courses, find it no easy task to stand before a class, demonstrate and explain techniques, and correct a number of other students.

Many causes contribute to this aspect of teaching; for example, in clubs where membership is comparatively small, it is not usual to have to use class teaching methods.

The practice of weight training is, however, growing considerably and the increasing number of enthusiasts will, at some stage, make it desirable to introduce the more conventional form of educational class teaching principles.

It is important to note here that it must not be assumed that this type of teaching is new to weight training: many clubs have been using these methods most successfully over a number of years.

Assessing capability

There are certain preliminaries to be observed before discussing in detail the advocated teaching sequence.

To any well read reader it is quite easy to appreciate the reasons why it would be most unwise to go headlong into a series of exercises with a pupil, unless some idea had been obtained about capability. It is of great importance to do this by testing each pupil on a series of fundamental exercises to establish the correct poundage to be employed.

Once this basic information is available, a series of suitable exercises can be drawn up. These exercises should be designed to exercise the muscle groups and joints over their full range of movement.

The soundness of the procedure will soon become apparent. Such a series of exercises is, principally, a conditioning course, and, therefore, is a foundation to progressing to the more advanced work of ability groups and specialisation, e.g. that used in individual training.

Class formation

Years of experience have taught the physical educationist that most apparatus work should be approached from a slightly different angle than that for free standing movements. First in teaching order should be class formation.

Class formation by the instructor depends, in the main, on the following factors: number of pupils; amount of space available; and quantity of apparatus. Although these divisions will be considered separately, it is important to remember that, invariably, all three factors will be applied in combination.

Number of pupils

It should be appreciated that to have the class arranged haphazardly causes a great deal of distraction among both pupils and other members, and means that control is difficult. Formation, therefore, depends on the space available.

Space available

Space available plays an important part in the formation of a class. For example, it may be convenient to arrange the pupils in a half-circle or in staggered teams. However, no hard and fast rule can be laid down and it is up to the instructor alone to arrange his pupils to suit the given circumstances, which may depend on the amount of apparatus.

Quantity of apparatus

This is also a variable factor. For a club with plenty of equipment the problem is simplified, because each pupil may possess a bar and necessary weights. With limited equipment, however, the principle of staggered team work would be the most advantageous system, since it is likely that only one set of weights would be available.

Having considered the general principles involved in class formation, there is one point which can be laid down very definitely, and which is applicable to any form of teaching. It is essential that the instructor places himself in such a position that he can see all his pupils and, conversely, that all pupils can see him.

To conclude this introduction, it is important to note that proficiency at class instruction will enable an instructor to teach individuals comparatively easily. However, this cannot be said of those who have never stood before a class of pupils.

Teaching sequence

The instructor is strongly advised to pay particular attention to mastering this sequence, because all candidates are required to demonstrate their ability to apply it with a class as part of the practical examination (B.A.W.L.A.).

In practice, the following sequence will also be found to be suitable when introducing a new exercise to more advanced students. The sequence will be considered under six headings:

1   Name the exercise
When naming exercises, keep the description concise. For example, assuming the press is being demonstrated, then say simply, 'This exercise is called the two-hands press.'

2   Name the major part of the body being exercised
The naming of muscles involved in a particular exercise often gets both instructor and student into difficulty. The description should on no account be technical and candidates are advised simply to name the major part of the body being exercised. For example, refer to the shoulders, lower back, front of the upper arms and so on, but avoid the use of Latin names.

Combining 1 and 2, keeping the press as the exercise, say 'This exercise is the two-hands press, mainly for the arms and shoulders.' At this stage make quite sure the attention of the class has been achieved; if it is necessary to issue a command, such as 'Look this way', never resort to the parade ground tone. The command must be firm, but friendly.

3   Give a silent demonstration in good style
The demonstration should always be given in the best possible style – if you desire the best results from instruction. What sort of response comes from the pupils depends entirely on what the instructor is prepared to give. The demonstration should be short and snappy, but note that this does not mean rushed. Finally, a reminder on repetitions: keep the number down to 2 or 3.

4   Give a demonstration and explanation
A very important warning: on no account must this be a lecture and it must commence from the starting position. To emphasise the point, consider the following examples. The half snatch, used as a warming-up exercise, commences from the floor; the two-hands press commences from the shoulders; the two-hands curl commences from the thighs; and so on. It should be borne in mind every time before this stage is begun.

To continue with the press as an exercise, all movements to the shoulders are the preambles. Detail the exercise from the starting position, giving a demonstration and explanation of each point. Again, two or three repetitions will suffice. It was stated above that the explanation must not be a lecture. If the instructor wishes to add further comment, it should be restricted to when the movement has been described: he can refer briefly to any common fault peculiar to the exercise.

5   Talk class into starting position
It will be remembered that for any given exercise there is a definite starting position.

Using the press as an example once more, the exercise commences from the shoulder. Movements prior to this position are the preamble. The preamble is very important to the instructor, because it gives an excellent opportunity to coax the pupils into the starting position. The introduction to the press, therefore, may run along the following lines. 'Insteps under the bar, bend the legs and grip the bar, knuckles forward and hands spaced slightly wider than shoulder width. Pull the bar strongly, and with a slight dip of the body, let the bar come to rest at the shoulders.'

After a little practice, and provided the instructor understands the exercise he is teaching, no difficulty should be experienced when coaxing the pupil into this stage of the sequence.

Afterwards the number of repetitions should be stated and the command to commence should be given. Attention is drawn here to the discussion in the previous section on the use of the voice, because at this stage the tone of the voice will play an important part in how the movement is carried out. A word of warning: if the pupils are rank beginners, it may be necessary for the instructor to do the exercise as well, since they may never have handled weight training equipment previously.

6   Coach and encourage

This final stage must always be carried out quickly and cheerfully, otherwise pupils may complete the number of repetitions given before the instructor gets started.

Avoid the common fault of rattling off all the major faults in the form of a monotonous list. Careful discretion must always be exercised when making any comment, no matter how small, and in any case the golden rule is that if anything has to be said, then make it positive and constructive.

Remember, the prime duty of an instructor is to coach, encourage and coax the pupils in his care into doing the exercise that has been set. Telling a class of pupils what to do is comparatively easy, but getting them to do it is far harder.

In conclusion, an excellent demonstration can be carried out and a clear and concise explanation can be given, but an instructor will have failed if his pupils do not perform the exercise correctly.

It is appreciated that many movements demand a greater degree of skill and co-ordination to perform than others, which often take considerable time to perfect. Provided, however, the instructor has developed the ability to spot mistakes quickly, and that he coaches positively and encouragingly, then experience will soon reduce these problems to a minimum.

If it is necessary to criticise, frame the criticism in terms of encouragement, because everybody thrives on such coaxing, especially when it is really deserved!

Technique of teaching ability groups

As stated in the preceding section, class teaching is suitable for beginners and for the introduction of new exercises. It is now proposed to consider the pupil who has passed through the earlier stages of weight training and about whose capability and all-round strength something is known.

Grouping of pupils

Division into groups is made by the elementary expedient of placing pupils into relevant sections where a similarity in strength and ability has been attained. This system has many natural advantages and one or two points will be discussed in detail.

Weight changes on apparatus is very often a difficult problem and should always be kept to a minimum if unnecessary distraction is to be avoided. By dividing the pupils into ability groups, this desirable principle can be catered for to a large degree because the division is based on similarity of ability and so the object of minimising weight changing is, in a relative sense, almost automatically achieved.

Further ability groups can be an excellent medium for coaxing weaker pupils, the principle being to create a desire to progress to a more advanced group. This application is most important and the instructor should always be prepared to pay considerable attention to correct placing of pupils among those of similar ability so as not to dishearten them. The problem is always encountered when dealing with a mixed class and positive action is needed if the groups are to be a success.

Basic groups

Remember, it is assumed in this discussion on ability group methods that pupils who have already completed a weight training course are being considered.

Generally speaking, the students will be familiar with the standard weight training exercises and it will no longer be necessary to 'spoon feed' them with demonstrations and unnecessary explanations. They can be arranged in their respective groups and the instructor need only call out the exercise to be performed, give the necessary instruction, 'Carry on', and immediately begin to walk round. He can give concisely worded corrections, plus the ever needed encouragement. To maintain interest as fully as possible, it is good practice to announce the next exercise to be carried out before the present one is completed. Within a few months of training on this system it will be necessary to divide the pupils further for more advanced training.

Types of group

There are many groups into which the instructor could place his pupils, depending entirely, of course, on the purpose in mind, e.g. postural cases, beginners, novice

and intermediate weight trainers and weight lifters. An instructor of an established club is therefore invariably faced with the supervision of groups of different standards. He should try to delegate the most competent performer of the group the pleasant task of assisting in supervision, thereby making him free to move from group to group.

Group discipline

To teach ability groups successfully, it is essential to have a methodical system. All weights and bars should be kept in the same place all the time and should be returned tidily when each training period is completed. By adopting this procedure a sense of orderliness and neatness will develop which will reflect the standard of performance in the various groups.

Furthermore, it is also a great help in fostering good club discipline and it then becomes a pleasure to work in an atmosphere of ordered and enthusiastic application.

Technique of teaching individuals

In preceding sections, class teaching was recommended when introducing newcomers to weight training exercises and ability group training was discussed for those pupils with some experience. The stage has now been reached when the principles for individual coaching can be brought in. It is proposed to base the discussion on the use of competitive movements known as the Olympic set. Now the knowledge of the instructor is put to the test. No longer can he generalise; every detail must be analysed, major faults corrected and even smaller points ironed out.

Preliminary introductions as a preamble to exercises or lifts as advocated for class teaching may be dispensed with, and a conversational tone of instruction can be adopted in their place.

Let us assume the lift being practised is the two-hands press. The instructor simply tells the pupil to perform the lift, stating the number of repetitions to be carried out. Careful attention is given to position work and technique, and the instructor waits for the bar to be returned to the floor. This, of course, only applies to the first repetitions and is a point not often grasped by instructors. It is most important to remember that criticism and corrective measures should on no account be hurried, because even with a weightlifter of considerable experience the first few repetitions will seldom be 'in the groove'.

Spacing for advanced pupils

Spacing of advanced students is important and must be planned carefully. When a pupil reaches a stage at which he needs individual coaching, it must be remembered that a great deal of concentration is required to co-ordinate correct technique of advanced movements.

Generally speaking, a platform is the ideal set-up for the Olympic lifts or, failing this, an area suitably marked out. Only the actual performer should appear on the platform or area. Remaining pupils should, preferably, be seated or should stand well clear of the performer.

The instructor must be positioned so that he has unrestricted vision, and he should be able to move around freely.

Teaching principles

Once again, it is necessary to remind the instructor that the voice must be used in a friendly, but firm, manner.

Faulty movements in technique must always be corrected by positive coaching. This often takes the form of assisting pupils by timing the command to fit the drive. However, a word of caution is needed. The instructor should be extremely careful when using such methods, because calling out even fractionally at the wrong time can completely upset the pupil's movement co-ordination and concentration. Practice, however, will soon enable the instructor to give assistance at the right time, although the pupil should be encouraged to learn to time himself inwardly so that he can summon the necessary fire at the correct moment – which is needed for advanced technique. Remember, when on the platform in competition, the lifter is on his own. Through positive coaching, paying regard to detail, plus the excitement of the event, the lifter should be able to do his best.

It must never be forgotten that everyone thrives on a few well chosen words of encouragement, and a pupil will usually respond to this by showing improvement and increasing faith in his instructor.

To sum up: the instructor must watch critically for faults, but he must always remember that his pupils are human beings. He must be ready to give sound advice, together with a valid reason for any change in style advocated, and by firm and stimulating coaching he should be able to help his pupil reach his full potential.

BASIC WEIGHT TRAINING TERMS

Before discussing the general terms, it is necessary at the outset to clear a common source of confusion between the use of 'weight training' and 'weightlifting'.

Fundamentally, the raising of a weight may, whatever the purpose, be considered weightlifting. However, to meet the specialist needs of those in the field of recreation and remedial work, the reader is advised to sub-divide this further.

The following divisions will meet the weightlifter's general needs.

Weightlifting terms

General application

Here we are concerned with basic exercises designed specifically to exercise a muscle or muscle group over the full range of movement. This system is most suitable for obtaining a degree of general fitness and a reasonable physique.

Specialist application

This normally follows the above, i.e. when a suitable degree of experience has been achieved. It is employed, therefore, by people termed 'body builders' who follow a system of advanced methods to achieve muscular bulk and definition.

The needs of other sports

There is little doubt, if any, that most sporting activities demand a sound basic strength, with emphasis on certain muscular groups depending upon the event.

Specialist exercises can, therefore, be directed to increasing the power and efficiency of the principle group of muscles used in the particular event, thus assisting the athlete to improve his ability in the chosen sport.

The needs of the competitive weightlifter

It is quite obvious that just as the athlete undergoes specialist training, so does the competitive weightlifter who is concerned with displaying his strength, fitness, speed, technique and balance. For example, the movements most widely employed in contest are known as the Olympic set, comprising three lifts called the two-hands clean and press, the two-hands snatch and the two-hands clean and jerk. Three attempts are permitted on each lift. The competitor's best poundage recorded for each of the three lifts is added together to form a total. The total determines the placing in the competition.

Remedial application

This specialised application is designed to strengthen the muscles by gentle progression and to rehabilitate affected muscle or muscles to the previous strength. It may even be employed to take the muscles beyond their previous ability. Depending on the extent of the injury, this use of weights must be carried out under the direct supervision of, and never without the approval of, a medical officer.

Body building and weight training terms

Standard exercises and single sets

Standard basic exercises are normally used as a fundamental form of training, so providing an excellent guide to the pupil's capability for progressing to more advanced work.

Several exercises are chosen, each of which is repeated eight to ten times. Occasionally, certain exercises such as the deep knee bend and heels raising require slightly more repetitions.

Advanced or specific exercises

This type of exercise demands a greater degree of strength and technique to perform than the standard exercise, emphasis being placed on throwing greater resistance on the muscular attachment of insertion. Being specialised, this system should only be used as a follow-on from several months of training.

The sets system

This system is followed by pupils of relative experience. They repeat each exercise in three or four groups. This is beneficial both to strength and to muscular growth, because it allows more weight to be used than would be possible if, for example, thirty repetitions were done without a rest.

Strict exercising technique

This method is so fundamental as to be especially recommended at the start of an individual's career, the principle being never to sacrifice position for repetitions. Additional muscles must not come into play in order to assist the movement being performed. Thus, if the maximum number of repetitions cannot be completed in the correct style, then the weight is too heavy.

Cheating methods, assisted inner range work

It is essential that the term 'cheating' is qualified, since it is really a misnomer. The principle involved is to allow a heavier weight to be employed and to use a slight assistance movement to overcome the resistance of the additional weight. The resistance should be increased on the most difficult range of the exercise.

Flushing methods, multiset system

The principle of flushing is to use an increased number of repetitions on a muscle group. This is to keep it flushed full of blood in an effort to encourage growth. For example, assume it is intended to flush the biceps (on the front of the upper arm). Three variations of the curl exercise could be employed, repeating each exercise, perhaps, in three sets of eight repetitions and thus using nine sets of biceps muscle work to pack the upper arm with blood.

Peak contraction inner range work

The body is positioned in such a way that when the movement is completed, the greatest load will be on the inner range.

Alternate set system, alternate muscle group work

This system is similar to flushing, but differs in so much as the exercise for the front of the upper arm would be followed by an exercise for the rear of the upper arm. For example, the Curl exercise would be alternated with a Triceps exercise until three sets of ten repetitions of each has been performed. Once again achieving the benefit of keeping the blood concentrated in the same region.

Physiological sequence

It is very important that the body should be thoroughly warmed up before progressing to exercises which use up strength and energy, i.e. the body must be started off in low gear and exercises which involve the smaller muscle groups should follow, e.g.

Front squat

press behind neck, two-hands curl.

These may be succeeded by heavier back and leg work which employs the larger muscle groups. The body, now being correctly warmed up, will be able to cope quite easily with the heavier type of exercise.

Exercises which permit the legs to be rested can now be introduced, such as press on bench and pull overs at arms' length, i.e. any exercise that creates deep breathing.

Finally, the routine should be concluded with exercises that do not call for any degree of all-round strength, such as abdominal, calf or forearm work.

Description of muscles in exercise

In the section dealing with the teaching sequence in a class situation, it was pointed out that when referring to the muscles in-volved in an exercise the description must on no account be technical. By this is meant that the actual name of a muscle should be avoided and a generalisation should be employed.

For example, a description could run as follows (assume the exercise being performed is the two-hands curl): 'This exercise is for the muscles on the front of the upper arm.' Below will be found the more general basic exercises, together with a brief description of the principal muscle or muscles involved. Potential instructors should make themselves thoroughly familiar with all these exercises and descriptions.

High pull up A general exercise for warming up the body.

Power clean A massive power builder for all major muscle groups.

Two-hands press and press behind neck Shoulder, upperback, back of upper arm and side of chest.

Two-hands curl Front of the upper arm.

Deep knee bend or squat Legs, back and chest; improves heart and lung condition.

Front squat As for squat above, but with greater emphasis; leg muscles on the anterior aspect of the thigh; hip muscles.

Press on bench, wide grip Chest, front of shoulders and back of upper arm.

Press on bench, shoulder width grip Variation of above; more resistance on arms and shoulders.

Straight-legged dead lift Rounded back – muscles either side of the spine, buttock and back of upper leg.

Straight-legged dead lift Flat back – great resistance thrown on lower back and back of thighs.

Heel raising Calf muscles.

Bent forward rowing To chest – principally the upper back; to abdomen – principally the lower back; close grip – upper back and front of upper arms.

Single arm rowing Upper back, trunk and muscles on the front of the upper arm.

Upright rowing Shoulders, upper back and front of upper arms.

Straight arm pullover and bent arm pullover Front of chest, lower back and shoulders, stretch and mobilise the thorax.

Press with dumb-bells Arm, shoulders and side of chest.

Bent forward triceps press with dumb-bells Muscles at the rear of the upper arm.

Triceps bench press Muscles at the rear of the upper arm.

Lateral raise lying Chest and front of the shoulders.

Lateral raise standing Shoulders and upper back.

Lateral raise bent forward Back of shoulders and upper back.

Screw curl with dumb-bells Front of upper arm.

Side bend with dumb-bell (one only) Side of trunk and mid-section.

Trunk forward bend Rear of thighs, hips and lower back.

Hack lift Leg and hip muscles.

Standing triceps press with dumb-bells The muscles at the rear of the upper arm.

PHYSICAL FITNESS FOR WEIGHTLIFTERS

What is physical fitness?

The importance of this subject has already been stressed. There are two types of fitness: (i) general fitness for work or sport, and (ii) specific fitness for a particular sport, which in this case is weightlifting.

Weightlifters must be sufficiently fit to perform with maximum weights in competition (including recovery between lifts), and must be able to withstand and recover from the heavy load volume and stress in training.

The following fitness 'factors' apply to weightlifters.

1   **Muscular power:** this is the combination of speed and strength to produce fast weightlifting movements. Explosive work, especially of the legs, enhances muscular power.

2   **Muscular strength:** this is seen in the lifter's capacity to overcome the resistance of the barbell. This handbook contains various ways of developing the appropriate form of applied strength necessary for weightlifting.

3   **Muscular endurance:** weightlifting training involves local muscle endurance. Muscles have to contract or maintain contractions in conditions of fatigue. Muscular endurance can be improved through training which improves circulatory processes by increasing capillarity. Weightlifters with high muscular endurance are able to tolerate better oxygen debt (anaerobic) effects.

4   **Cardiovascular endurance:** this is general endurance or stamina. Efficient cardiac, vascular and capillary actions are required for improved weightlifting and faster recovery between lifts or exercises. To improve cardiovascular efficiency, the lifter must perform aerobic activities three times a week during which time his pulse rate should be raised to at least 130 beats a minute and maintained at that level for at least 10 minutes. A choice of jogging, high repetition weights' work, circuit training and interval running provide the basic training for the heart and lungs.

5   **Skill:** co-ordinated neuromuscular pathways are necessary for the development of good technique. Coaching and practice are important for the attainment of this factor.

6   **Flexibility:** efficient execution of the fast lifts requires adequate range of movement at joints. A weightlifter has to incorporate mobility work in his training. Free exercises, pair work, barbell work and other apparatus may be used. The aim is to counteract short muscles, fascia and ligaments.

Differences between the physically fit and unfit

To understand the reasons why a weightlifter should undergo fitness training, the following comparison between physically fit and unfit persons should be studied.

1 For easy work that both can sustain in a steady state.	Fit	Unfit
(a) Oxygen consumption	lower	higher
(b) Pulse rate during work...	lower	higher
(c) Stroke volume during work	larger	smaller
(d) Blood pressure during work	lower	higher
(e) Blood lactate	lower	higher
(f) Return of blood pressure to normal after work	faster	slower
(g) Return of pulse rate to resting value after work	faster	slower

2 For exhausting work that neither can sustain in a steady state.	Fit	Unfit
(a) Maximum oxygen consumption	higher	lower
(b) Maximum pulse rate during work..	usually lower	usually higher
(c) Stroke volume	larger	smaller
(d) Duration of work before exhaustion	longer	shorter
(e) Return of blood pressure to normal after work	faster	slower
(f) Return of pulse rate to resting value after work	faster	slower

Summary of main benefits of fitness

There are many benefits of physical fitness for a weightlifter.
They include:

1 improved muscle tone
2 increased agility
3 improved mechanical efficiency
4 improved capacity for relaxation
5 increased ability for concentration during training and weightlifting competition
6 improved metabolic, physiological and possibly psychological efficiency; blood pressure is decreased and heart and breathing rates are lowered
7 Weightlifting performance can increase because a greater degree of fatigue can be endured and recovery is quicker in the fit person than in the unfit individual.
8 General feeling of well-being.

Conclusion

Weightlifters must include fitness training in their programmes. Attainment of fitness involves a change of physiological state with improved efficiency. The process takes time and cannot be achieved in a few training sessions. In practice, a good deal of time is given over to cardiovascular and other fitness work in the early part of the preparatory period. This is reduced in the competitive period and is emphasised again in the transitional period.

Physical fitness terminology

Aerobic training is used for the improvement of general endurance. The training effort varies from moderate to high intensity. With aerobic training the lifter has sufficient oxygen for his output. The greater the cardiovascular reserve of the lifter, the higher is his aerobic capacity.

Anaerobic training is characterised by efforts of maximal or submaximal intensity whereby sufficient oxygen is not available for the lifter's neuromuscular output. The anaerobic performance lasts for a few seconds or less, as in the speed or strength performances. The aerobic effort depends on the lifter's capacity to tolerate the 'oxygen debt' (q.v.) involved. This type of training is necessary for the development of muscular energy.

Steady state is the term used to describe the situation when a lifter's oxygen intake and consumption are kept at a steady level, with waste products being oxydised as they occur.

Oxygen debt: In performances involving bursts of great strength or speed, the oxygen intake is insufficient to meet the demands of the body. The lifter is said to incur an oxygen debt. In some cases less than 25% of the inhaled oxygen passes into the blood and the working muscles. Excess fatigue products, principally lactic acid, are produced and spill over into the blood by 'buffering reactions'. In the recovery phase after the intense activity these fatigue products are oxydised, or in more common terms the oxygen debt is repaid. It is possible to reach such a high level of lactic acid that muscles can no longer contract, there-by limiting performance. Thus it follows that weightlifters need to develop a high oxygen debt tolerance.

Vital capacity of the lungs is the largest quantity of air a person can forcibly expel from his lungs after the deepest inhalation possible. It is sometimes known as Forced Vital Capacity (F.V.C.). Vital capacity is thought to be closely related to body weight and body surface area. In addition, there is evidence to suggest that there is a relationship between physical work and vital capacity. The ratio FEV 1 sec/FVC (Forced Expiratory Volume at 1 second divided by Forced Vital Capacity) is a useful measure of lung efficiency.

Dynamometer is an instrument used to measure muscular strength. For example, gripping strength is measured by means of a grip dynamometer.

Goniometer is an instrument used to measure the range of movement at a joint. In its simplest form it consists of a protractor with a movable arm. There are also electronic goniometers (or ELGONS) which measure joint flexibility in motion.

Spirometer is an instrument used to measure vital capacity.

WEIGHT TRAINING

Weight training employs the principles of progressive resistance or the overload system. This means that muscles are progressively overloaded to improve strength response, which in turn has beneficial effects on speed and, consequently, power.

Weight training can be employed for a number of reasons. It is now an integral part of all modern sports preparation, because there are real advantages to be obtained from this type of training. It may take a variety of forms using different sorts of apparatus. However, in this book we look at free apparatus, i.e. barbells and dumb-bells. It must be remembered that the range of exercises is far greater with such apparatus than with machines. If you learn the exercises illustrated in this book, you will certainly be able to coach weight training with fixed apparatus.

Coaches should study the sections on anatomy and kinetics in order to understand the basic requirements of sports and various activities and to be able to prescribe the correct exercises.

In this section there are two programmes. One is for general weight training and the other is for a specialist sport (cycling). They show how a year's work is organised.

From these examples it should be possible to prepare other programmes to suit individuals' needs.

Basic weight training course

Objectives

To develop fitness through strength, mobility and cardio-vascular improvement. Before each workout, warm up thoroughly with freestanding exercises as follows.

1 Gentle running on the spot, gradually increasing tempo. 1 minute, increasing to 2 minutes as fitness is developed.
2 Arm and shoulder mobility – arm circling.
3 Trunk mobility – trunk twisting.
4 Trunk and hip flexion – knee raising – trunk bending.
5 Hamstring stretching. Very gentle toe touching.

Apart from being used as part of the warm up, these exercises are especially valuable in exercising the joints over their full range, thereby improving mobility.

Basic programmes

These are based on an 'A'–'B' schedule programme. Each schedule is alternated session by session. This ensures that a fully comprehensive range of exercises can be used and that there is variety in the programme. The exercises are designed to be performed with bar bells and dumb-bells. Also given are equivalent exercises for the trainer who has access to fixed apparatus.

Choice of weight

The ultimate choice of weight to be used for each exercise will depend upon the previous athletic history of the trainer and his age and weight. To start with, use 'token weights', i.e. weights that are sufficiently heavy to ensure exercise, but light enough for the trainer to learn the movements and to become accustomed to the new type of exercise. After a short while the trainer will soon know the type of resistance that can be handled.

Programme

Weeks 1–4
Objectives
To learn movements; to develop mobility and basic strength; to increase the pulse rate.

SCHEDULE A	Suggested weight lb	(kg)	SCHEDULE B	Suggested weight lb	(kg)	Fixed apparatus (equivalent)
Warm up			*Warm up*			
High pull up	30	(15)	Power clean	30	(15)	
Press behind neck	30	(15)	Press from chest	30	(15)	Seated press
Two-hands curl	30	(15)	Two-hands curl	30	(15)	Pulley curl
Bent forward rowing	30	(15)	Single D/B rowing	10	(05)	Pulley rowing
Back squat	45	(20)	Front squat	45	(20)	Leg press
Bench press	45	(20)	Bench press	45	(20)	Bench press
Side bend	10	(05)	Side bend	10	(05)	Pulley side bend
Abdominal work	FREE		Abdominal work	FREE		Abdominal work

The straight arm pullover can be used as an alternative to bench pressing. Both the exercises need some assistance.

Weeks 5–8
Objective
To build up strength and fitness.

SCHEDULE A	SCHEDULE B
Warm up thoroughly	*Warm up thoroughly*
High pull up	Power clean
Press behind neck	Press from chest
2-hands curl	2-hands curl
Bent forward rowing	Bent forward rowing
Press on bench	Press on bench
Back squat	Front squat
D/B side bend	D/B side bend
Inclined abdominals	Abdominals with weights

The above programmes should be completed as follows:

WEEKS 1–4	WEEKS 5–8
Schedules A + B, alternately, 3 minimum, preferably 4 times a week	Schedules A + B, alternately, 3 minimum, preferably 4 times a week
Resistance to be handled	
As shown above (p. 110)	Based upon his experience during the first four weeks the athlete will know the amount of weight that he can handle for each exercise. This will now be heavier as he employs the principles of progressive resistance.
Repetitions	
10 – first two weeks 12 – 3rd week 15 – 4th week	Repetitions will be related to the increase in weight and will now be 8 for each exercise, except abdominal work. For this exercise 4 sets of 15 repetitions should be performed.
Sets of repetitions	
2 sets of each exercise (repetitions as above)	Each exercise should be completed for 4 sets
Rest periods	
	No longer than 1½ minutes
In order to overload the cardio-vascular system, rests should be short, no longer than 1½ minutes	No longer than 1½ minutes

Weeks 9–12

Objective
To develop power and fitness.

SCHEDULE A	SCHEDULE B
Warm up thoroughly	Warm up thoroughly
High pull up or power snatch	Power clean
Heave press	Heave jerk
2-hands curl	2-hands curl
Bent forward rowing	Bent forward rowing
Press on bench	Press on bench
Back squat	Squat jumps
D/B side bends	D/B side bends
Advanced abdominals	Advanced abdominals

The above programmes should be completed as follows:

Schedules A and B, alternately, 4 times per week.

Resistence to be handled

The resistance can be considerably increased during this period. It will mean that the repetitions will be lower in the heavier sets, as illustrated.

Repetitions	8	6	5	4	3	3
Sets	1	2	3	4	5	6

The weight should be increased set by set. Remember: do not sacrifice good exercise technique for extra weight.

For exercise – dumb-bell side bends, 4 sets of 8 repetitions.
For abdominals – 4 sets of 20 repetitions.

Rest Periods
No longer than 1½ minutes.

Throughout the programmes, with the exception of the first three weeks, the work load has remained at approximately 30 repetitions per exercise. The progressive development has come through the increase in the resistance to be handled and by keeping the work time to the minimum.

Progressive resistance training – example (cycling)

From the outset it is important to be aware that there are limitations as well as advantages in progressive resistance training. The use of weights is obviously not the panacea for all the deficiencies that may occur in a cyclist's make-up, and even as an enthusiast I would be a fool to try to convince you that this is so. I hope that I can show the real advantages of this form of training, rather than the imagined ones.

I believe that the use of weight training for the cyclist has three main functions, and that these are:

1 To be used as part of the general build-up of fitness and endurance. This is related specifically to the period of the event and to the rapid recovery from the physical stress of this period of activity. It is also related to the general ability to complete, with success, the training plans as presented during the week, or as required prior to competitions.

2 To develop power in the form of strength and speed training to enable the cyclist to master, with ease, the essential skills of the activity. Often skill will be limited to a low level, because the participant does not have the basic strength and power necessary for the mastery of the skill. Closely related to this is mobility. Mobility can be developed and maintained, and the strengthening of a muscle, over its full range of movement, is an essential aspect of a fitness programme.

3 To develop and strengthen muscles, and ligaments, resulting in the minimisation of joint injury and the more rapid rehabilitation of previously injured points to full playing capacity.

In preparing a plan of progressive resistance exercises for an athlete, it is important to have these fundamental objectives clearly in mind. All too often one comes across training plans, which include schedules, where the needs of the athlete have not been fully understood. The general and specific requirements of the event, and the time of the year, or season, are covered, blanket-fashion, often with complicated exercises and extended workouts that are more suited to the weightlifter or bodybuilder than to the athlete only concerned with using weights as an assistance for his own sport. The type of weight training planning required by a heavy field athlete will obviously differ considerably from that employed by a games player. The cyclist is concerned with being a better cyclist, not with becoming a weightlifter.

As previously stated, the application of weights can be used to produce several end results. These are:

1 fitness of a general nature
2 specific endurance
3 strength

4   speed
5   power.

In order to achieve success, these qualities must exist to a lesser, or greater, degree in all activities.

In the case of the first-class cyclist, it might be reasonable to assume that the fitness and endurance aspects of the activity are taken care of by the general nature of the club-training regimes. Weight training programmes would not, therefore, be concerned with the development to any great degree of these qualities. This emphasis may shift with the training of competitors of lower standards, and more concentration on 'weights for endurance' would be employed. For what purpose, then, will progressive resistance work be included in the training of the first-class cyclist? Empirical analysis of the event shows a need for power in the mastery of these skills, which involve the following essential basics:

1   very rapid change of pace
2   maintenance of burst pace
3   high level of endurance/power for long distance events
4   bike control
5   prevention of injury through power/ mobility training and rehabilitation of injuries to full functional capacity.

Having decided for what purpose weights can be used, let us now consider the way in which they are used.

As previously stated, the benefits to a first-class cyclist of using weights for fitness and endurance only may well be limited. However, since cycling involves all these qualities as well as power, I will explain how they may be achieved.

Fitness

The type of exercises used in the fitness programme are those which employ large groups of muscles at any one time. The objective is to place great overload on the cardio-vascular system. Such exercises include power cleaning and snatching, high pull-ups, squats, lunges and bench pressing. All these exercises are of a massive nature.

The repetitions must be high. A resistance is chosen that will permit ten repetitions without the loss of form. As the participant finds it easier to perform the ten repetitions, so he progresses to fifteen and from there to twenty in easy stages. When the selected maximum is achieved, the weight is increased so that he can now achieve the required maximum.

Rest pauses between sets of repetitions and between exercises should be kept to the minimum. These pauses should only be long enough to permit the breathing to return almost to normal. By almost normal is meant a level which will not affect the skill or rhythm of the movement or skill. This, in actual time, is usually between thirty and ninety seconds maximum, depending upon the number of repetitions performed and the resistance used. Try to cut down on the length of the rest periods so that greater demands are made on the cardio-vascular system.

Endurance

Endurance training is an extension of fitness work. The number of repetitions can be considerably increased up to as many as fifty. The exercises chosen should still be of a massive nature, involving large muscle group complexes. The weights used should be light and high repetitions should be performed quickly, with as short a rest period between the exercises and sets as possible.

Strength and power training

When training for strength and power, the athlete adopts the opposite procedure to that employed in fitness and endurance training. Now he needs to use much heavier resistance and, consequently, lower repetitions. The resistance selected should not permit more than five repetitions to be performed for any exercise and the total number of repetitions should not exceed twenty-five. An exercise could, therefore, be performed for five sets of five repetitions.

At times it may be necessary to handle weights which permit only three or two repetitions, and the athlete may well go to singles, where maximum resistance is being handled. Exercises such as power cleans, high pull-ups and power snatch, upward jumps with heavy weights, heave presses and jerks with barbells and dumb-bells, cheating single-handed rowing, etc. are all good power exercises.

Speed

Successful speed training is dependent on increases in strength and power, since the athlete should have greater power than his activity limits demand. Speed is a quality whereby the muscles act against a given resistance, producing fast movements at a joint, or joints, far beyond normal action. The muscles must possess the strength to activate the joints against resistance set up by the body, part of the body, or some outside resistance in the shortest possible time. A combination of strength, power and light, fast movements blended with the athlete's own event will greatly improve speed.

The shot putter requires far greater power and speed than the actual resistance the 16-lb shot presents, and the tennis player needs great speed and power not only in striking the ball but also in the highly important change of direction and court cover, so that if necessary he is properly positioned to deliver maximum force in his stroke play. Reserves of speed and power will enable him to overcome with far greater ease the problems that the game and his opponent place upon him.

Since cycling varies so much in its nature, ranging from very long distance races that last over many days to all-out sprinting over very short periods of time, progressive resistance training will naturally be approached in a number of different ways. It should, however, be remembered that the main objective should be the development of power. The long distance cyclist will probably get quite sufficient endurance work from his training on the bike and so endurance/weight training may, in fact, be a waste of time. Indeed, such an athlete may well require power work with comparatively heavy weights to develop an aspect of his athletic make-up that might be otherwise neglected.

The short duration cyclist must concentrate on heavy power work; however, he might benefit from light weights with high repetitions, especially during the closed season, to build up local muscular endurance and a base upon which the heavier training can be developed later in the season.

This is progressive resistance training, so do not be afraid to advance the resistance being handled. Throughout the training period an athlete should aim for all-round bodily development, with specialist exercises being added later in the programme. Make sure that both you and your charges perform the exercises in strict exercise technique: do not sacrifice correct body position for weight; warm up thoroughly all the joint complexes before you start training with weights; and take at least two days' rest between heavy power training and competitive activity. Vigorous weight training can be very fatiguing and this should be recognised, especially as it involves local muscular endurance and can, therefore, affect skills if such sessions follow too soon.

Recovery time is essential in order to re-cuperate sufficient energy and power for your own speciality.

Planning the weight training programme

The requirements will differ for various parts of the year. The cycling coach needs to appreciate that the weight training plans and schedule have different values, depending upon the general training load placed upon the rider and upon the part of the season.

The programme can be divided broadly into the following sections:

1 close or non-participating phase
2 pre-season phase
3 start of season
4 throughout the season.

Close or non-participating phase

The best time to introduce weight training to the athlete is during the non-participating period of the year. This will give the coach the opportunity to follow a comprehensive schedule which will lay down a basis of all-body fitness, mobility and strength. The schedule will be general, employing exercises for all muscle groups. The repetitions will be high so that adequate stress will be placed on the cardio-vascular system and the resistance principle will be directed primarily to the increase of repetitions. This period should last from 3 to 6 weeks and there should be three training sessions per week. In the initial stages the resistance will be token only, but towards the end of this period the coach should have a very good idea of the weights that the cyclists should be able to handle in subsequent training phases.

Pre-season phase

For some 4 to 8 weeks prior to the start of the season the number of exercises will be cut down and those of a massive nature employed. The resistance is increased with a corresponding reduction in the number of repetitions and now the set system is used. Training at this time becomes specific in laying down strength and power. Again, the cyclist should train three times per week. This period should lead into the next phase.

Start of season phase

During this period for about 4 weeks a schedule aimed at power building should be employed. The exercises are of a massive nature, but now attempts can be made at maximums. This means that an exercise can be followed on the repetition basis of 5-4-3-2-1-1. When a number of sets and repetitions is decided upon, then there will be an increase in the poundage handled in each set, e.g. 1 set of 5 repetitions of 50lb, 1 set of 4 repetitions of 75lb, 1 set of 3 repetitions of 100lb, and so on. When the season has begun and the demands of the sport have increased, this period and the subsequent phase will involve training on two days per week only.

Full season

Once the season is in full swing, the objective is to maintain the basis of power that has been developed in the previous training periods. Again, the training will be on two days per week. Select good, general power exercises and a resistance sufficient to ensure that the repetitions are kept low. Then perform 5 sets of each exercise. This type of training can be followed throughout the season and should produce good results as far as maintenance of power is concerned. Since the use of weights is challenging in itself, do not be afraid to let the cyclists increase the poundage that they handle, provided they maintain the correct lifting technique at all times.

The chart on the next page gives a picture of the type of schedule and exercises to be used for the various training phases throughout the year.

CLOSED SEASON

**Learning, fitness, mobility
High pulse rate – short rest**

3 times per week
Mon   Wed   Fri

Exercise	Sets	Reps
High pull-up	1 set	10–20 reps
Press behind neck	1 set	10–20 reps
2-hands curl	1 set	10–20 reps
D/B side bend	1 set	10–20 reps
Bent forward rowing	1 set	10–20 reps
Back squat	1 set	10–20 reps
Power cleans	1 set	10–20 reps
Bench press	1 set	10–20 reps
Pullovers	1 set	10–20 reps
Abdominals	1 set	10–30 reps

3–6 weeks depending on existing
level of fitness

PRE-SEASON

Strength build-up

3 times per week
Mon   Wed   Fri

Exercise	Sets	Reps
Power cleans	4 sets	8 reps
Heave press	4 sets	8 reps
Back squats	4 sets	8 reps
'Good morning' exercise	4 sets	8 reps
Pull overs	4 sets	10 reps
Abdominals (with wt)	4 sets	10 reps

4–8 weeks

START OF SEASON

Power build-up

2 times per week
Mon   Wed

Exercise	Sets	Reps
Power cleans	5-4-3-2-1-1	
Bench press	5-4-3-2-1-1	
Squat jumps	3 sets	5 reps
Round back Dead lift	3 sets	5 reps
Pull overs	3 sets	8 reps
Abdominals	progressive	

4 weeks

THROUGHOUT SEASON

Power maintenance

2 times per week
Mon   Wed

Exercise	Sets	Reps
Schedule 'A' Monday		
Power cleans	5 sets	4 reps
Heave press	5 sets	4 reps
Pull overs	5 sets	4 reps
Back squats	5 sets / 2 sets	5 reps / 3 reps
Hyperextensions	Free	
Schedule 'B' Wednesdays		
High pulls (wide grip)	5 sets	4 reps
Squat jumps	5 sets	4 reps
Power cleans	5 sets	4 reps
Calf raises	5 sets	6 reps

Remaining playing time

Selection of weight to be handled

Because there are differences in the physical build of all individuals, it is not possible to be definite about the weight to be used. This will be decided by the athlete or his coach after the initial training period. At first a weight must be selected that will enable movements to be learned and yet will thoroughly exercise the participant. Weights in the range between 15 to 30lb will be suitable, depending upon the individual. You may find these to be very light, but remember that you have to work up to 20 repetitions and that you have to learn all the exercises. In subsequent training periods, weights can be adjusted to your own developing strength.

Sets and repetitions

The amount of work that an athlete is required to do is broken up into sets of a specified number of repetitions; for example, if a lifter decides that he needs to perform thirty repetitions of an exercise, his choice will be between the development of endurance or of strength. For endurance he might complete the thirty repetitions in one set without any rest. This means that the weight would have to be light. On the other hand, because one of the main objectives of weightlifting training is to develop strength, the resistance handled must be increased. Naturally, he could not perform one set of thirty repetitions, so the exercise is performed over three sets of ten repetitions or six sets of five or, at a more advanced level when the resistance is very heavy, ten sets of three. This is known as the set system of training.

Warming up

Before any weight training it is essential that a short warm-up period of free standing exercises is followed. These include those that you will have learned whilst at school, and should include full range mobility work for all the major joint complexes of the body.

WEIGHTLIFTING SAFETY

Safety for teachers and coaches

Every teacher wants to prevent accidents in physical education. Accident victims may suffer physical and psychological injury and distress which may impair future happiness. The P.E. programme may be cut back and all sorts of restrictions may be introduced. Teachers, coaches and authorities may also suffer stress and loss by being sued for negligence and damages if students are injured while using defective equipment, if there is inadequate supervision or if reasonable care is not taken by the person in charge.

To protect your pupils, your employers, your programme, your budget, and YOURSELF, give full consideration to the recommendations set out below.

General physical education

1 Have all equipment inspected regularly. Report in writing all deficiencies in apparatus, mats, floor surfaces, rigs, equipment, etc. to your superior. Don't use until put right. *Get the best equipment and keep in good condition.*

2 Make sure you have taught all the necessary *skills*, including safety procedures, before requiring students to exercise them in game, class or competition situations.

3 Get medical approval before putting an injured student back into game, class or competition activity. *Get and follow medical advice.*

4 Beginners need special teaching and supervision. A champion trying out an entirely new skill is a beginner at that skill. *Supervision means being there when needed.*

5 Fatigue often precedes accidents. Students must be fit, at the time, for the work to be attempted. *A tired pupil is often accident prone.*

Weight training and lifting

In addition to the above, *keep the apparatus locked up unless at least* THREE *people want to use it.*

1 Ensure that your lay-out for the different exercises in the weight training area is carefully planned. Barbells should not be too close to each other. Use mats under the weights. Transport of equipment requires great care. *Do not permit horseplay.*

2 Check the barbells, stands, benches, dumb-bells, etc. carefully before use. Make sure all collars are tight and barbells are evenly loaded. Check the apparatus each time it comes out and after every set: *it is your responsibility.*

3 Only train in an area where the floor is even, firm and non-slip. Do not permit individuals to train in bare feet. *Balance in progressive resistance training is very important.*

4 Check and service your equipment regularly: *it's good insurance.*

5 Know WHY and when to teach specific exercises, as well as how. Good intentions are no excuse for ignorance. *Attend an official coaching course.*

6 Make sure that stand-ins (two) are used for all exercises, one each side of the barbell ready to assist. Teach all pupils how to stand-in and catch. *Ensure that the stand-in knows when and how to help.*

7 Ensure that pupils do not attempt limit poundages too soon. *Too great a weight = bad body position = accident.*

8 Teach exercises carefully. Ensure strict exercise principles are employed at all times. *Every pupil must advance at his own level.*

9 Use only token resistance during the exercise learning phase. When muscle groups are weak, they lack control. Lack of muscular control can lead to injury. *Proceed with caution and always with careful supervision.*

10 Correct breathing on all lifts must be taught. *Apply correct training principles.*

11 Encourage the use of warm clothing in which to train and fast training procedure to avoid 'local chilling' of muscles. *Employ correct training principles.*

12 Before driving your pupils on to advanced training schedules or to competitions at too early a stage in their career, analyse your motives. Unless the well being and safety of the performers come above personal vanity and ambition, it could be a dangerous programme. *Integrity is the keyword to remember when supervising pupils.*

13 Display a notice in the gymnasium and ensure all students are familiar with the recommendations. Have your rules and enforce them. *Stay in charge.*

Safety for pupils and competitors

Weight training, i.e. strength and muscle building, is a very worthwhile end in itself. It assists in the development of skill acquisition and is an important aspect of any physical fitness programme. The sport of weightlifting is exciting, requiring great speed, strength, mental control, fitness, courage and mastery of technique. Many top athletes employ progressive resistance principles in their training.

The use of weights, however, requires careful thought. The skills of the activity must be learned very thoroughly. Poor technique, reckless advancement of poundages and irresponsible behaviour can cause accidents. Pupils should listen to their coach or teacher and should apply the correct training principles, while coaches should respect the limitations of each individual. Everything should be clear before training is started.

An injury may result from somebody else not thinking, but if you think and behave responsibly you will never hurt yourself or anybody else. *Consider the following.*

1 Confidence should not be confused with recklessness; the former is built on knowledge, the latter on ignorance. *The only impression reckless weight training makes is on the floor.*

2 Although weight training and weightlifting are great fun, because you can see and take pride in the progress you are making, to become an expert still takes time – time spent on understanding and mastering each step before moving on to the next. *Don't 'try to run before you can walk'.*

3 Before trying the next exercise or training plans and schedules, get and follow advice from your teacher or coach. *The teacher's or coach's job is to ensure that all the experiences you will have from the use of weights will be pleasant ones.*

4   *Never train alone*: always have one stand-in at each end of the bar. *The stand-ins should know what you are going to do and when.*

5   Keep to your schedule of exercises. Do not advance to poundages without your coach's advice. *Do not sacrifice correct body position for poundage.*

6   Do not try to keep up with others who may seem to be making more rapid progress than yourself. Train at your own level and within your own capabilities: *you will make progress.*

7   Horse play and practical jokes can be very dangerous. *If you are not getting enough fun out of serious weightlifting work, it's a poor programme.* Wear firm training shoes and warm clothing.

8   Check all apparatus before use and after each exercise. Check collars. Make sure they are firmly secured. Make sure all bars are evenly loaded. *Concentrate and be safety-conscious.*

9   When you begin thinking about competition lifting, you will need to have followed a sound training programme. Technique must be mastered. Strength and power building must be developed steadily. *Your success in competition will depend upon a controlled and progressive approach to training.*

EXERCISES

Get set or starting position

Starting position
Feet should be hip width apart under the bar. Feel the weight of the body over all of the feet. Bending at the legs and hips, grasp the bar, maintaining a flat and strong back. (*See photograph 1.*)

Movement
Maintain the flat back position, with the arms straight. By straightening the legs, stand erect. The lifting is done by the legs and hips – the strongest part of the body. (*See photographs 2 and 3.*)

Breathing
Breathe in as you raise the bar and out as you lower to the get set or starting position.

Purpose
This is the method that must be employed in all lifting movements, whether it is when using barbells, dumb-bells, boxes, buckets of coal or suitcases. Use the strong muscles of the legs and hips to overcome the resistance. Keep the back flat and strong at all times. Learn this skill first; it is very important and will greatly contribute to the elimination of back injuries which result from incorrect lifting procedures.

1. Get set position

2. The back is kept flat

3. The arms are kept straight throughout the lift

High pull-up 1. Starting position

2. The bar is pulled high in a regular rhythm

High pull-up

Starting position
Assume the get set starting position. (*See photograph 1.*)

Movement
Pull the bar high. Note the position of the wrists and the elbow, and also of the chest – it is high and the hips are slightly forward as the body comes up high on the toes. Repeat in a brisk, non-stop rhythm. (*See photograph 2.*)

Breathing
Breathe in as you raise the bar, and out as you lower to the starting position.

Purpose

With light weights this movement is useful as a warming-up exercise. However, with heavier weights it is a real all-round power builder.

Two-hands press

Starting position

The bar rests on the top of the chest. Use shoulder-width hand spacing. The body is braced strongly. (*See photograph 1, p. 124.*)

Movement

Maintaining the body in a strong, firm position, the barbell is driven above the head to arms' length. (*See photograph 2.*)

Breathing

Breathe in as the barbell is driven above the head and out as it is returned to the starting position.

Purpose

The exercise develops the muscles of the arms, shoulders and sides of the trunk.

Seated press

Starting position

Begin in the seated position. The barbell rests on the front of the shoulders. (*See photograph 1, p. 123.*)

Movement

The barbell is pressed strongly from the chest to above the head. (*See photograph 2.*)

Breathing

Breathe in as the barbell is driven above the head and out as it is returned to the starting position.

Purpose

Because the lifter is seated, the action is isolated to the arms and shoulders.

Press behind neck

Starting position

Feet astride, with the bar resting comfortably behind the neck. (*See photograph 1, p. 126.*)

Movement

Press the barbell straight to arms' length overhead. (*See photograph 2.*)

Breathing

Breathe in on the upward movement and out as you return to the starting position.

Purpose

To develop the upper back muscles, muscles of the shoulder and those at the rear of the upper arm.

Two-hands curl

Starting position

Note that the body is vertical, the arms are straight and the palms are to the front. (*See photograph 1, p. 127.*)

Movement

Bend the arms strongly at the elbows until the bar rests on the chest. Make sure that the bar is kept close to the body. (*See photograph 2.*)

Finishing position (*see photograph 3*)

Note that the elbows are fully flexed, yet are still behind the bar, thus keeping the resistance on the muscles concerned. Should you bring the elbows forwards and upwards, you will take all the resistance away and will defeat the object of the exercise.

By varying the grip on the bar, from a wide grip to a very close one, or by changing the position of the trunk, the effect of the exercise can be altered.

Breathing

Breathe in as you raise the bar and out as you lower it.

Purpose

To develop the muscle on the front of the upper arm.

Left Two-hands press 1. Starting position. *Below* 2. Driving the barbell above the head to arms' length

Opposite (top) Seated press 1. Starting position. *(bottom)* 2. The barbell is pressed above the head

Press behind neck 1. Starting position

2. The barbell is pressed above the head to arms' length

Top left Two-hands curl 1. Starting position. *Top right*
2. The elbows are bent and the bar is brought up to the chest

3. Finishing position for the two-hands curl

Upright rowing

Starting position
Bend down, grip the bar (knuckles to the front and hands approximately 8 inches apart) and stand up. The bar should now be hanging at arms' length against the top of the thighs. This is the starting position. (*See photograph 1, opposite.*)

Movement
Pull the bar up the front of the body until it reaches the height of the chin. (*See photograph 2.*)

Breathing
Breathe in as the bar is raised and out as you return it to the starting position.

Purpose
To develop the muscles surrounding the shoulders and upper back, as well as the muscle which flexes the elbow.

Variation
In a 'cheating' version, the legs may be used slightly to help the exerciser handle heavier weights.

Power cleans with barbell

Starting position
The legs are well bent, but the back is flat. (*See photograph 1, opposite.*)

Movement
Extend the legs and back vigorously, bringing the arms into action as the barbell passes the mid thighs and finishing in the receiving position. (*See photograph 2.*)

Breathing
Breathe in as you lift and out as you lower the barbell to the starting position.

Purpose
To develop all-round body power. This exercise can also be done with dumb-bells.

Bent-forward rowing

Starting position
The back is flat, the head is up, the arms are straight, the knuckles are to the front, the hands are fairly wide apart, the feet are wide astride and the knees are slightly bent. (*See photograph 1, p. 130.*)

Movement
Pull the bar strongly to the chest, by bending the arms and raising the elbows sideways. Lower the barbell under control. (*See photograph 2.*)

Raised position
This shows the position as the bar touches the top of the chest. It is excellent exercise for improving shoulder posture. Note that the body has not moved during the movement.

Breathing
Breathe in as the bar is pulled to the chest and out as the weight is returned to the starting position.

Purpose
Principally, to develop the upper back muscles. The effects of this exercise can be altered by bringing the bar up and back to touch the lower abdomen. This affects the lower back muscles.

Squat (or full knee bend)

Starting position
Feet are comfortably apart, normally hip width, with the bar resting across the upper back. (The heels may be raised on blocks of wood 1½ inches high.) (*See photograph 1, p. 130.*)

Movement
Bend the knees and squat down. Gently rebound out of the low position and rise strongly by lifting the head; at the same time strongly straighten the legs. (*See photograph 2.*)

Upright rowing 1. Starting position

2. The bar is brought up in front of the body to the chin

Power clean with barbell 1. Starting position

2. Receiving position

Bent forward rowing 1. Starting position

2. Lowering the barbell under control

Squat (full knee bend) 1. Starting position

2. Bending the knees and squatting down

Low position

The back is flat, but is not vertical. This position elevates the ribs and has a stretching effect on the thorax, which encourages chest growth. The squat can be used with many variations for the legs, or as a general power builder. Due to the larger groups of muscles being used, a great demand is made on the circulatory and respiratory systems, which greatly encourages increasing body weight. The squat is the keystone of many weight training schedules. Should you find difficulty in keeping the back flat as you approach the low position, it is advisable either to avoid going all the way down or to put a chock of wood under the heels about 1½ inches high. This throws most of the resistance on the front of the thighs.

The effects of this exercise can be greatly altered by the extent to which the exerciser bends his legs. Several hundred pounds can be used in shallow or half squats.

Breathing

Fill the lungs, bend the knees, breathe out just as you rebound in the low position and you will find that the air is driven out of the lungs. Breathe in as you rise.

Purpose

To develop the legs, back and chest, and to improve the condition of the heart and lungs. *Note:* in most cases it is neither necessary nor advisable to go lower than in the illustrated position.

Vertical or squat jumps

From a half-squat position, leap upwards, putting as much effort as possible into the drive from the legs. Be sure to land on the toes. Bend the knees to take the shock out of landing. Make sure you are well balanced before each repetition. This variation develops an explosive leg action and also develops the muscles of the hips, the front of the thighs and calf muscles.

Front squats

Starting position

Feet are comfortably apart, normally hip width, with the bar resting across the upper chest. (*See photograph 1, p. 132.*)

Movement

Lower the body into the full squat position. (*See photograph 2.*) Vigorously extend the legs and return to the upright standing position.

Breathing

Breathe out as you bend the knees and in as you rise to the standing position.

Purpose

To develop mainly the muscles on the front of the thighs and the hip muscles.

Lunges or split squats

Starting position

Take up the position with the front leg stepped well forward, the rear foot pointing straight ahead, the heel raised, and the bar held high on the chest. Make sure that your balance is perfect before attempting the movement. (*See photograph 1, p. 132.*)

Movement

Lower the body and the weight from this position by bending both legs. (*See photograph 2.*) Note that the forward knee should be in advance of the forward foot. The direction of the lunge can be altered with each repetition, as can the leading leg. For example, first repetition directly forward, recover feet together, changing leading leg, lunge to side, recover feet together, changing leading leg, lunge to opposite side, and so on.

Breathing

Breathe as freely as possible during the exercise.

Purpose

To build power and mobility in the legs. This exercise is especially valuable to all

Left Front squat 1. Starting position. *Above* 2. The full squat position

Lunge or split squat 1. Starting position

2. Full lunge position

racket games players and in those sports where quick change of direction is essential.

Heave press

Starting position
Pull the barbell from the floor to the chest, dip the body by bending the legs and assume the starting position. (*See photograph 1, p. 134.*)

Movement
Extend the legs and arms vigorously; finish the last half of the movement in the correct pressing style. (*See photograph 2.*)

Breathing
Breathe in as you extend the arms and legs, and as you lower the bar to the starting position. As this is a power movement, it is often necessary to breathe in and out a few times between repetitions at the shoulder.

Purpose
To produce collectively power and development in the arms, shoulders and legs. Muscles involved are the extensors of the arms and legs, and the shoulder flexors and elevators of the shoulder girdle. This exercise can also be performed with dumb-bells.

Press on bench

Starting position
Lying with the back on the bench. The bar should be resting on the chest, the fore-arms should be vertical below the bar, and the hands should be wide apart. (*See photograph 1, p. 135.*)

Movement
Press the barbell vigorously to arms' length. (*See photograph 2.*)

Breathing
Breathe in as you press the bar upwards and out as you return it to the chest.

Purpose
To develop the chest muscles, front shoulder muscles and muscles on the back of the upper arm.

Variation
This exercise can be performed by supporting the bar across the lower chest, hands shoulder-width apart, arms close to the side of the chest. This variation throws a greater resistance on the arms and shoulders.

Trunk forward bend

Starting position
Assume feet-astride position, with the bar resting comfortably behind the neck. (*See photograph 1, p. 136.*)

Movement
Bend forwards from the hips, keeping the back flat, but allow the knees to bend slightly as the trunk comes horizontal to the ground. (*See photograph 2.*)

Breathing
Breathe out as you bend forwards and in as you return to the starting position.

Purpose
To develop the muscles at the rear of the thighs and hips and the lower back muscles.

Straight-arm pull-over

Starting position
Lying on the back on a narrow bench. The barbell is held at arms' length. (*See photograph 1, p. 137.*)

Movement
Keep the arms straight and lower the bar in a quarter circle backwards until you reach the position shown in the illustration, or even lower down. (*See photograph 2.*)

Stretch position
In the early stages, it is advisable to keep the lower back flat on the bench, and the weight light. A good point to remember in all straight-arm movements is the advisability

of performing the first two repetitions in slow, steady time to make sure the muscles are stretched over the full range before you attempt the exercise at full tempo.

Breathing
Breathe in as you lower the bar and out as you return to the starting position.

Purpose
To enlarge the thorax and to develop muscles surrounding the shoulder girdle as well as the muscles on the front of the chest and the large muscles of the lower back.

Heave press 1. Starting position

2. The legs and arms are extended vigorously

Press on bench 1. Starting position

2. The barbell is pressed to arms' length

Trunk forward bend 1. Starting position

2. Bending forwards from the hips

Variation
The bar may be started from a resting place across the thighs.

Opposite (top) **Straight-arm pull-over** 1. Starting position

Opposite (bottom) 2. The bar is lowered in a quarter circle

Bent-arm pull-over 1. Starting position

2. The bar is raised from the chest, directly backwards over the head

Bent-arm pull-over

Starting position
Lying back on a bench or form, with the bar resting on the lower chest. A narrow grip should be used and elbows should be at the sides. (*See photograph 1.*)

Movement
Raise the bar off the chest and directly backwards over the head until it reaches the illustrated position. Try to keep the elbow joints at right angles throughout the movement. (*See photograph 2.*)

Breathing
Breathe in as the bar goes backwards and out as you return the bar to the chest.

Purpose
To stretch and mobilise the thorax, and to develop the chest muscles and the large muscles of the lower back.

Variation
A centrally loaded dumb-bell may be used.

Standing triceps press with dumb-bell

Starting position
Feet astride, with the dumb-bell lowered behind the neck. (*See photograph 1.*)

Movement
Vigorously straighten the elbow until the dumb-bell is above the head. (*See photograph 2.*)

Standing triceps press with dumb-bell 1. Starting position

2. The elbow is straightened so that the dumb-bell is above the head

Dumb-bell press 1. Starting position

2. The dumb-bells are pressed to arms' length overhead

Breathing
Breathe in as the dumb-bell is raised and out as it is lowered.

Purpose
To develop the muscles at the rear of the upper arm.

Dumb-bell press

Starting position
Grip two dumb-bells, one in each hand; bring the bells to the shoulders (*see photograph 1*).

Movement
Press the dumb-bells evenly to arms' length overhead, keeping the body in the starting position throughout. As you drive the bells from the shoulder, lift the chest high (*see photograph 2*).

Finishing position
The chest is held high and the body is in a strong upright position, with the elbows straight and the arms vertical. Dumb-bell work has a great strengthening effect on the muscles. This is especially true of the overhead exercises, as they are much more difficult to control than the barbell.

Breathing
Breathe in as the bells are pressed overhead and out as the bells are returned to the starting position.

Purpose
To develop the shoulder muscles, upper back muscles and the muscle at the back of the upper arm.

Alternate dumb-bell press

Starting position
The dumb-bells are cleaned to the shoulders. The body is well braced (*see photograph 1, p. 142*).

Movement
Start the movement by pressing one of the dumb-bells (with the weaker arm) to arm's length. As the dumb-bell is lowered, rock the body slightly to the opposite side whilst pressing the opposite dumb-bell to arm's length (*see photograph 2*). The dumb-bells should pass each other at approximately the mid-point of the movement. Perform this exercise rhythmically.

Breathing
Breathe as freely as the exercise permits.

Dumb-bell bench press

Starting position
Lying on the bench, as for bench press, dumb-bells pointing fore and aft and held close to the shoulders.

Movement
Press the dumb-bells to arms' length. Lift shoulders at the finish of the movement.

Breathing
Breathe in as the dumb-bells are pressed upwards and out as they are returned to the starting position.

Purpose
To develop the muscles on the front of the chest and shoulders. At the final part of the movement considerable resistance is thrown on the muscles at the back of the upper arm.

Alternate dumb-bell bench press

Starting position
Take up the same starting position as for the dumb-bell bench press.

Movement
Begin with the right arm: press the dumb-bells to arms' length alternately. As the one is lowered, so the other is pressed. They should pass each other about mid-way.

Alternate dumb-bell press 1. Starting position

2. The dumb-bells are each pressed rhythmically to arms' length

Breathing
Breathe freely throughout this exercise.

Purpose
To develop the muscles of the arms and shoulders. This exercise is especially important for those involved in pushing and punching movements.

Dumb-bell screw curl

Starting position
Stand erect, with the feet a few inches apart. The dumb-bells should be hanging at arms' length, with the rear end of the disc pointing forwards. (*See photograph 1, p. 144.*)

Movement
Bend the arms strongly at the elbows; as the bells reach the midway position, turn the rear ends in towards each other. Keep the elbows from coming too far forwards at the completion of the curl. (*See photograph 2.*)

Finishing position
The body is erect and the elbows are still behind the bells; this is important to keep the resistance on the muscles being used.

Breathing
Breathe in as the weights are raised and out as you return to the starting position.

Purpose
To develop the muscles of the front of the upper arm.

Dumb-bell side to side bend

Starting position
Stand astride a dumb-bell, bend down and pick it up with the right hand, and assume the illustrated starting position. (*See photograph 1, p. 145.*) Keep the body square to the front.

Movement
Bend the body strongly to the right as far as possible. (*See photograph 2.*)

Finishing position
Note how the body has kept to the lateral plane.

Breathing
Breathe in as you raise the weight and out as you return to the starting position.

Purpose
To develop the muscles on the sides of the trunk and numerous other muscles surrounding the mid-section.

Single-arm rowing

Starting position
Feet astride, legs bent, and one hand supported on a low bench. The dumb-bell hangs vertically beneath the shoulder. (*See photograph 1, p. 145.*)

Movement
Pull the dumb-bell strongly from the starting position to a point close to the side of the chest. (*See photograph 2.*)

Breathing
Breathe in as the bell is raised and out as you return to the starting position.

Purpose
To develop the upper back muscles, the trunk and muscles on the front of the upper arm.

Cheating single-arm rowing

Starting position
Take up the position illustrated, keeping the back as flat as possible. (*See photograph 1, p. 146.*)

Movement
Pull the dumb-bell vigorously up into position. (*See photograph 2.*) Rotate the trunk so that the chest is facing sideways and upwards. Keep the free hand on a low chair or stool. This should not be higher than 1ft (0.3m) above the floor.

Dumb-bell screw curl 1. Starting position

2. The elbows are bent strongly

Dumb-bell side to side bend 1. Starting position

2. The body is bent strongly to the right

Single-arm rowing 1. Starting position

2. The dumb-bell is brought towards the side of the chest

Cheating single-arm rowing 1. Starting position

2. The dumb-bell is pulled up vigorously

Breathing
Breathe in as you raise the dumb-bell and out as you return to the starting position.

Purpose
To develop the muscles which rotate the trunk and also those of the shoulder and upper back.

Triceps bench press with dumb-bells

Starting position
Lying back, with dumb-bells held as in the illustration. (*See photograph 1.*) Note the backward angle of the arms and the tilt back of the bells. The bells are supported by the little finger side of the hand resting against the inside of the front disc.

Movement
Keep the upper arm still as you lower the bells into a position behind your head. (*See*

photograph 2.) Drive the bells straight back to the starting position, making sure they never come vertically over the shoulders. This keeps the resistance on the triceps muscles.

Lower position
Care should be taken in lowering the bells from the raised position. Note the elbows are well bent and pointed high. The hands are close to the inside of the front discs.

Breathing
Breathe in as the bells are raised and out as they are lowered.

Purpose
To develop the muscles at the back of the upper arm.

Opposite (top (1.) *and bottom* (2.)) Triceps bench press with dumb-bells

Bent forward triceps press with dumb-bells 1. Starting position

2. Both elbows are extended, while the body and shoulders remain still

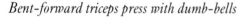

Bent-forward triceps press with dumb-bells

Starting position
Feet astride, knees bent. Lower the chest close to the upper thighs, keeping the elbows pointing upwards. (*See photograph 1.*)

Movement
Hold this position and extend both elbows. The body and shoulders are to be kept still during the movement. (*See photograph 2.*)

Breathing
Breathe freely throughout the movement.

Purpose
This is a very strong exercise to develop the muscles at the rear of the upper arm.

Lateral raise lying

Starting position
Lying back on a narrow bench or form. Dumb-bells are held at arms' length vertically over the shoulders. (*See photograph 1.*)

Movement
Keep the arms straight and lower the bells sideways until they are approximately below the level of the shoulders. Comparatively light weights must be used for this exercise. (*See photograph 2.*)

Breathing
Breathe in as the bells are lowered and out as the bells are returned to the starting position.

Purpose
To develop the chest muscles and muscles on the front of the shoulders.

Opposite (top) Lateral raise lying 1. Starting position *(bottom)* 2. The bells are lowered sideways

Lateral raise standing 1. Standing position   2. The dumb-bells are raised sideways

Lateral raise standing with dumb-bells

Starting position
Assume the feet-astride position, with the dumb-bells resting against the thighs. (*See photograph 1.*)

Movement
Raise the dumb-bells sideways. Raise the chest high at the same time. Lower and repeat the movement. (*See photograph 2.*)

Breathing
Breathe in as you raise the bells and out as they return to the starting position.

Purpose
To develop the shoulders and upper back muscles.

Bent-forward lateral raise standing

Starting position
Knees slightly bent, and back flat and horizontal to the ground. (*See photograph 1.*)

Movement
Maintain the starting position of the back and legs and raise the dumb-bells sideways to a point slightly above the level of the shoulders. (*See photograph 2.*)

Breathing
Breathe in as you raise the bells and out as you return to the starting position.

Purpose
To develop the abductors of the scapula and muscles which cap the shoulder joint.

Bent forward lateral raise standing 1. Starting position

2. The dumb-bells are raised sideways

Above Single dumb-bell, alternate swing 1. Starting position. *Right* 2. Transferring the dumb-bell from the right hand to the left hand

Single dumb-bell, alternate swing

Starting position
Feet slightly wider than hip width. The dumb-bell is held in one hand between the legs. Knees are bent back flat. (*See photograph 1.*)

Movement
The dumb-bell is swung upwards and forwards to a level with the face. This is achieved by a vigorous extension of the legs, hips and back. At the top of this position, (*see photograph 2*), the dumb-bell is transferred to the opposite hand and is allowed to swing back down (under control) to the starting position. This is performed in a rhythmical manner.

Breathing
Breathe in on the action of swinging the dumb-bell upwards and out as it is allowed to swing back down.

Single dumb-bell clean

Starting position
Feet slightly wider than hip-width, and dumb-bell pointing fore and aft. Bend down, keeping the back flat, and grasp the dumb-bell with one hand. (*See photograph 1.*)

Movement
Vigorously straighten the legs and lift the dumb-bell, turning it over to catch it at the shoulder. (*See photograph 2.*) Raise the opposite arm to the horizontal position as a counter-balance.

Breathing
Breathe in as the dumb-bell is lifted and out as you return to the starting position.

Purpose
To develop all-round power. Both arms must be exercised.

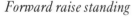
Above Single dumb-bell clean 1. Starting position. *Right* 2. The legs are straightened and the dumb-bell is lifted and caught at the shoulders

Forward raise standing

Starting position
Body upright, feet hip-width apart, dumb-bells resting across the thighs. (*See photograph 1, p. 154.*)

Movement
Keeping the arms straight, raise the dumb-bells forwards to a point slightly above the level of the shoulders. Keep the chest high throughout the movement. (*See photograph 2.*)

Breathing
Breathe in as the dumb-bells are raised and out as you return to the starting position.

Purpose
To develop the muscles at the front of the shoulders.

Straight arm pullover with dumb-bells

Starting position
Lying on the bench, as for bench press. Let the dumb-bells rest on the thighs, pointing upwards, and keep the arms straight. (*See photograph 1.*)

Movement
The dumb-bells are taken from the starting position in a semi-circle to a position behind the head at arms' length. (*See photograph 2.*)

Breathing
Breathe in as the dumb-bells are raised (and take to the position behind the head) and breathe out as they are returned to the starting position.

Purpose
To develop the muscles of the chest, lower back and shoulders. It also elevates the rib cage.

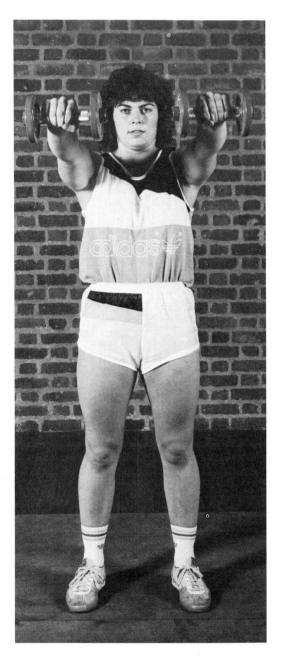

Forward raise standing 1. Starting position

2. The dumb-bells are raised slightly above the shoulders

Straight arm pull-over 1. Starting position

2. The dumb-bells are taken behind the head in a semi-circular movement

Abdominal curl 1. Feet are held by a partner

2. The trunk is 'curled' until the elbows are close to the knees

Abdominal exercise

Starting position
The feet are fixed under a bar or, as illustrated, they are held by a training partner. The knees must be slightly bent and the hands must be clasped behind the head. For the very inexperienced, the hands can be placed on the thighs.

Movement
From the starting position, sit up, curling the trunk until the elbows come close to the bent knees. (*See photograph 2.*) Alternatively, sit up and slide the hands along the thighs.

Breathing
Breathe out as you sit up and in as you return to the starting position.

Purpose
To develop the muscles of the abdomen and side of the trunk and those that flex the hip.

This exercise has many variations depending upon the experience of the trainer. Feet may be raised, as on an inclined abdominal board, and a weight may be held behind the head during the movement. Such manoeuvres will greatly increase the resistance to be overcome.

INDEX